Investing in the Age o

Morten Arisson

Investing in the Age of Democracy

Ten Lessons in Applied Austrian Economics

Morten Arisson
Credit Portfolio Manager
Toronto, ON, Canada

ISBN 978-3-319-95902-3   ISBN 978-3-319-95903-0   (eBook)
https://doi.org/10.1007/978-3-319-95903-0

Library of Congress Control Number: 2018949926

Cover credit: GettyImages/REB Images

This Palgrave Macmillan imprint is published by the registered company Springer Nature Switzerland AG
The registered company address is: Gewerbestrasse 11, 6330 Cham, Switzerland

To Jennifer, Victoria and Benjamin

Disclaimer

The comments expressed in this book are my own personal opinions only. I wrote and marketed this book as an independent activity, outside my regular work. No part of the compensation I receive from my employer was, is or will be directly or indirectly related to any comments or personal views expressed in this publication. All comments are based upon my current knowledge. You should conduct independent research to verify the validity of any statements made here before basing any decisions upon those statements. The information contained herein is not necessarily complete and its accuracy is not guaranteed. The comments expressed in this book provide general information only. Neither the information nor any opinion expressed constitutes a solicitation, an offer or an invitation to make an offer, to buy or sell any securities or other financial instrument or any derivative related to such securities or instruments. The comments expressed in this publication are not intended to provide personal investment advice and they do not take into account the specific investment objectives, financial situation and the particular needs of any specific person. All rights reserved.

Contents

List of Figures

Introduction

In his work *Politics*,[1] Aristotle describes what could have been an established political view in Ancient Greece: That we are constantly involved in a self-perpetuating cycle of political change, consisting of six types of government. Three of these types were called "regular": Monarchy, aristocracy and democracy.[2] And they had their respective corrupted versions: Tyranny, oligarchy and demagogy. We must bear in mind that when Aristotle wrote, he had the privilege of knowing, from written form or orally, the political history of his ancient world, probably dating back to the early times of Egypt. This suggests that our political developments up to date are incredibly regular, even though we are constantly reminded that we live in unique times (Fig. 1).

The age of democracy, as I refer to in this book, began with the American and French revolutions. Like other revolutions before and after, they were both nurtured and defended by intellectuals; and they set off a sequence of developments that would define how we invest in the twenty-first century. The resulting paradigm and the process that took us here are the subject of this book.

The direct result of these two revolutions was a global expansion of democratic regimes that is still taking place, although with different cultural and regional characteristics. But the rise of democracy did not take place in a vacuum. In spite of it, we improved our living standards, triggering an

---

[1] *Πολιτικά*, Aristotélēs; 384–322 BC.

[2] The suffix "-archy" stems from Greek's "arkhia", which meant "rule". Monarchy is the rule of one, that is, "monos". Aristocracy and democracy stem from the words aristos-kratia or the power of the aristos, that is, the best, and demos-kratia or the power of the people.

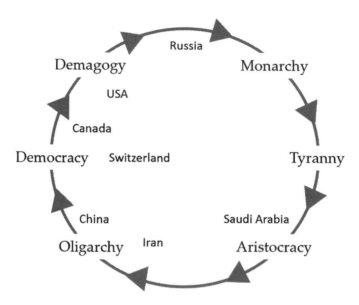

Fig. 1 Aristotelian types of government: pure and impure

exponential growth in the world's population. From a metaphysical[3] stand-point, before the rise of democracy and to this day, the adoption of the scientific method by the social sciences (and Economics and Finance are some of them) has been indiscriminate. One can trace here the perennial influence of Gottfried Leibniz.[4] Together with the population increase, "scientism"[5] put forth the idea that central planning of and for a society can be done and must be tried. The impact of scientism and central planning on how we make investing decisions today is represented by the careless use of probability theory, differential analysis and general equilibrium theory. Another direct result of scientism is the search of efficiency and the negligent application of optimization and mathematical programming in Humanities.

At the very core of the rise of democracy lies the problem of sovereign financing. With the collapse of the feudal system, taxation had to be both widespread and painless. It had to be widespread because it had to finance constant expansion: The American, French and later Bolshevik revolutions

---

[3] Metaphysics or "beyond physics" is a branch of philosophy whose subject study is the structure, nature and fundamental principles of the "real world".

[4] Gottfried Wilhelm Leibniz (1646–1716), one of the most influential philosophers of the modern age.

[5] The word scientism is used to describe the indiscriminate use of the scientific method in all fields of knowledge. Scientism has been dealt with extensively by the brightest minds of the twentieth century. For the purpose of this book, I will simply say that the scientific method is inadequate to study our actions, because they can never be objectively observed according to precise parameters and, above all, the observations are not repeatable but constitute a series of historical unique events.

were (and in the case of the American still are) expansionist. And it had to be painless because, from now on, those being taxed had a vote too. This combination has always forced democratic governments across geographies and generations to monetize their fiscal deficits. But eventually, as the quality of the sovereign credit monetized and sold to banks deteriorated, these fell prey to recurrent crises. Their bailouts had to be financed with notes enforced upon depositors first and entire populations later. These notes became legal tender and their issuing institutions, central banks.

The cocktail of scientism and central banking opened the door to the idea of central planning. Once this idea was taken seriously, it was only natural to witness an increasing interest in the use of statistics and probability theory. The latter suffered a mutation that has also influenced how we invest today. From its origins and until the twentieth century, the study of probability had been focused on collective phenomena and had therefore been established within what would later be formally recognized (in Mathematics) as finite spaces. But in the early twentieth century and particularly after J. M. Keynes' *Treatise on Probability* of 1921, the theory shifted away from the study of the observable, into a subjective discipline. This shift was tangible and originated in all likelihood from misinterpreting the work on the law of large numbers published by S. D. Poisson in 1837. Had it been properly understood, modern portfolio theory would have probably never existed.

With the rise of democracy, the ideas of government and property had to change too, by definition. Law was dropped in favour of legislation, in a trend that had set off in the Middle Ages but took a definitive turn first with Grotius in the Netherlands of the seventeenth century and later in France with Bonaparte. A few decades later in Prussia and under Bismarck, collective savings were enforced on citizens for the first time. And in July of 1844, with the Peel Banking Act in Britain, fractional reserve banking was legitimized and the right of depositors to redeem their property became an aleatory variable[6]: It is only possible as long as one outsmarts other depositors, redeeming one's property first.

Because of its obvious social consequences, multiple remedies to cloak the weakness of fractional reserve banking have been attempted. They resulted in increasing degrees of violence against property. The first was the creation of central banks. In the United States, this was followed two decades later by the expropriation of private money in 1933, through Executive Order 6102.[7]

---

[6] J. Huerta de Soto, Chapter III, *Money, Banking Credit and Economic Cycles, Third English Edition, 2012.*

[7] Signed on April 5, 1933, by President Franklin D. Roosevelt. It forbade the possession of gold coin, gold bullion and gold certificates within the continental United States by private individuals.

This state of affairs lasted until in 1971 fiat money was finally fully imposed.[8] The next step will likely be the prohibition of cash, to protect the reputation that there is at stake with Basel III.[9] The steady invasion on property rights unfolded in parallel (and enabled in many ways by technological progress), with a deliberate intrusion on privacy. The notion that rulers can and should have full knowledge of one's wealth, as long as they rule in democracy, is now completely acceptable.[10] In aggregate, these political developments have had strong repercussions on how we invest. We have developed instruments to serve the needs of aggregate, collective investing entities, totally disregarding its unintended consequence: The surge of what is commonly known as systemic risk. In the process, we also redefined the concept of sovereign risk.

Lastly, as a result of the steps taken since 1971, the notion of liquidity was also corrupted. When J. M. Keynes wrote about liquidity in 1936, he still referred to it from a subjective point of view. He properly called it liquidity preference. Today, liquidity is rather considered an attribute intrinsic to a market. When players refer to a market as liquid, what they implicitly mean is that leverage is available to transact in that market, without a genuine saving counterpart.

In the following pages, I propose an approach to investing in the face of the aforementioned issues. These define an era where investing has been increasingly shaped after five factors: The misuse of infinitesimal calculus and probability theory, the ignorance of entrepreneurial knowledge, a disregard for the role played by institutions in the market process, a confusion between the

---

[8] With Executive Order 6102, gold was confiscated to use it as reserve in support of the US dollar, at an exchange rate of $35/oz. This rate was however a benchmark, as redemption of gold from the US government, by all relevant means, was prohibited to individuals. However, gold continued to trade in the rest of the world, and by 1971, it was clear that the exchange rate of $35/oz could no longer be sustained. On August 15, 1971, President Nixon put an end to the nominal convertibility of the US dollar. This action was a simple acknowledgement of a reality that could no longer be hidden. However, for all practical purposes, it meant that we could no longer hope to return to the use of private money, as had been the case for thousands of years. From then on, money would be replaced by enforced legal tender, the sovereign credit of the United States.

[9] Basel III is the name commonly given to the group of regulations for financial institutions put in place after the 2008 crisis. Quantitatively, these regulations force banks to increase their liquidity and capital. Qualitatively, they simplify the capital structure and end up firmly validating the double standard "depositors" face. In good times, they will be called depositors. In bad times, they will be forced investors, as they have to bail in their banks. Their deposit contracts have an element of *alea*. Basel III affected the profitability of banking, while at the same time, it protected the market position of the most established institutions. The involved fixed compliance costs constitute a barrier to entry in the sector.

[10] As Prof. Miguel A. Bastos Boubeta notes, an invasion of privacy to that extent would have been difficult under monarchies prior to the French Revolution. The monarchs themselves knew their governments were not fully legitimate and therefore could not afford to be hated. Today, under the garment of legitimacy that dresses democratic regimes, privacy is simply a luxury of the past.

concepts of money and capital (and therefore interest rates), and the lack of an appropriate theory of the business cycle.

My suggested approach to investing is based on five conceptual pillars: A proper understanding of entrepreneurship and institutions, a rediscovery of probability theory as conceived originally by Bernoulli and Poisson, the notion of intertemporal exchange (and its connection to dynamic asset allocation), the distinction between money and capital, and a brief discussion on economic growth and cycles.

Bibliography

Aristotle. (n.d.). Politics. University of Chicago Press, March 29, 2013. Retrieved from Google Books June 2015 from https://books.google.ca/books?id=DJP44Go myNoC&lpg=PP1&pg=PP1#v=onepage&q&f=false

Russell, Bertrand. (1946). History of Western Philosophy. London: Unwin University Books.

Keynes, John Maynard. (1921). Treatise on Probability. London: Macmillan & Co., Ltd.

Poisson, Siméon Denis. (1837). Recherches sur la probabilité des jugements en matière criminelle et en matière civile, précédées des règles générales du calcul des probabilités. Paris: Bachelier Imprimeur-Libraire. Retrieved August 2015, from https://www-liphy.ujf-grenoble.fr/pagesperso/bahram/Phys_Stat/Biblio/Poisson_Proba_1838.pdf

Huerta de Soto, Jesús. (2006). Dinero, Crédito Bancario y Ciclos Económicos. Madrid: Unión Editorial, 6ta Edición, 2016.

Bastos Boubeta, Miguel Anxo. (2013). Libertarianismo y Conservadurismo. VIII Universidad de Verano, Instituto Juan de Mariana, retrieved August 2015, from: https://youtu.be/NzZJipDVd9o

David, Florence N. (1909). Games, Gods and Gambling: A History of Probability and Statistical Ideas. Mineola, NY: Dover Publications Inc., 1988.

Part I

The Current Paradigm

1

Working with the Wrong Tools

In *The Problem of China*,[1] Lord Russell quotes a certain Mr Chi Li,[2] on the influence of hieroglyphic writing upon education and ways of thinking:

> *… The accumulative effect of language-symbols upon one's mental formulation is still an unexploited field. Dividing the world culture of the living races on this basis, one perceives a fundamental difference of its types between the alphabetical users and the hieroglyphic users, each of which has its own virtues and vices…*

The above analysis leaves us with an interesting conclusion: Our ways of thinking or "mental formulations" are affected by the tools we use to express our ideas. And I would suggest to the reader that the way we look at financial and investing issues is affected by the tools we use. Since the 1870s, six innovations have developed that shaped what we know today as Theory of Finance. They underlie the way we approach investing, but in my view, they also constitute fundamental fallacies. In no particular order, these are (1) the use of differential analysis, (2) the use of general equilibrium theory (dealt with in the Appendix section), (3) the use of probability theory, (4) the (corruption of the) concept of liquidity, (5) the misunderstanding of sovereign risk and, by transitivity, (6) the risk of contagion, also known as systemic risk or correlation.

---

[1] B. Russell, 1922, George Allen & Unwin Ltd.

[2] "Some Anthropological Problems of China", Chinese Students' Monthly (Baltimore), for February 1922.

© The Author(s) 2018
M. Arisson, *Investing in the Age of Democracy*,
https://doi.org/10.1007/978-3-319-95903-0_1

Differential Analysis

Every paper in the Theory of Finance and most algorithmic trading strategies today are based on differential analysis. However, the assumption that human action (of any kind, not just limited to investing) takes place in continuous form is erroneous. It is an assumption that cannot pass the slightest test of reality. The "taste" for continuity dates back to the origin of infinitesimal calculus,[3] to Gottfried Leibniz (1646–1716).

This mathematical concept, as useful as it is in other fields, is misleading when applied to human action and, therefore, to investing. Infinitesimal or minimal changes in the context in which we unfold entrepreneurial behaviour do not produce infinitesimal results. I may have a business, and if the government increases my capital gains tax rate from 15% to 16% during one year, I will probably not change a single process or decision in my daily operations. It can happen again two years later, taking the rate from 16% to 18%, and still although I will get concerned and think twice before making capital expenditures, most likely, nothing will have changed with the way in which my business operates. But if five years after the first increase, another hike takes the tax rate on capital gains from 18% to 21%, it is likely that a whole new front of opportunities will open, with tax advisers cold-calling me to discuss how to reorganize the legal structure of my company. And a significant wave of mergers, acquisitions, asset sales, spin-offs, capital outflows or conversions may ensue, taking policy makers by surprise, as they end up collecting less revenue from this tax at a 21% marginal rate, than previously, when they charged only 15%.

Why did I not react before the 21% tax rate was imposed? Probably because the cost of seeking advice or reorganizing the legal structure of the company was too high to justify change at a 15% or 18% rate. And probably too, other entrepreneurs in the tax-advisory sector saw that as well. However, at a 21% rate, perhaps suddenly these entrepreneurs came up with a cost-effective marketing strategy, and once they began discovering the new market opportunity, reorganizations became a no-brainer.

This is simply one of the infinite examples that illustrate how we react to small changes. **Inertia does not just belong to the world of physics. It is also omnipresent in human action. We only change the status quo after**

---

[3] Leibniz was one of the creators (the other one was Sir Isaac Newton) of differential and integral calculus, and is quoted to have said "*Natura non facit saltum*" (i.e. nature does not make a jump). According to Lord Russell, this would have been no coincidence, as Leibniz "*was a firm believer in the importance of logic, not only in its own sphere, but as the basis of metaphysics*". His view on natural phenomena eventually spread to other scientific environments, to the extent that in *Principles of Economics*, Alfred Marshall chose the same quote as epigraph.

we realize that the cost of maintaining it is higher than that of changing it. In the meantime, we do not react. We put up with discomfort as long as our appreciation of the cost of getting rid of it is higher than its benefit.

One can legitimately ask why we use infinitesimal calculus in Finance and Economics. When a paradigm is incorrect, two consequences follow: First, a wrong paradigm leads to wrong conclusions. And second and most important, when we are comfortably using a wrong paradigm, we refrain ourselves from discovering the correct one.

In Finance (and in Economics too), the assumption of continuity gives a false sense of reality.[4] What underlies and is vitally connected to this assumption is the misunderstanding of the concept of liquidity, which I deal with later in this lesson.

Human action unfolds in leaps; it is discreet, not continuous. It has to be so, because we face eternal uncertainty, not risk. Risk is bounded, like Cauchy[5] put it, *"between the given limits"*. Uncertainty knows no a priori limits. And it is the recognition of this that drove humans to develop institutions, to coordinate behaviour and thus, over time, to come up with the *"given limits"*. The proof that our actions cannot be described in continuous time, with continuous functions, using infinitesimal analysis is in the fact that we use money. If life was ruled by continuities, bounded by limits, we would have developed institutions to barter. But we do not barter. We trade indirectly, through an institution that we call "money".

Probability Theory

The ability to use probability in Finance is the least challenged axiom that I have encountered. The theory of probability itself is also relatively recent, more recent than the study of Finance. Like most breakthrough innovations, the study of probability began as an applied discipline. Nobody knows exactly when it did, but there is a consensus that the first attempts were initiated by

---

[4] Perhaps a clear example of this is the indiscriminate application of delta-hedging strategies that defeat the whole purpose of having a hedge: To protect from abrupt and unforeseen changes (*"The delta of a derivative is defined as the rate of its price with respect to the price of its underlying asset,"* John Hull, *Options Futures and Other Derivatives*, Ch. 14.5, 3rd edition). Option pricing using the Black-Scholes model, based on differential equations, in the long run converts any serious hedging exercise into failure. In spite of this, not even the collapse of the Long-Term Capital Management Fund in 1998 was sufficient to discard continuity.

[5] Baron Augustin-Louis Cauchy (France, 1789–1857) pioneered the development of analysis. Formalization properly of continuity was elaborated in the early nineteenth century by Bernard Bolzano (1817) and Augustin Cauchy (1821). In Cauchy's words a function f (x) *"is continuous with respect to x between the given limits if, between these limits, an infinitely small increment in the variable always produces an infinitely small increment in the function itself."*

Girolamo Cardano (1501–1576), who among other things was a gambler. Later on, Pierre de Fermat (1601–1665, lawyer), Blaise Pascal (1623–1662), Jacob Bernoulli (1654–1705), Pierre Simon Marquis de Laplace (1749–1827) and Siméon Denis Poisson (1781–1840) established the basis for the comprehensive work that blossomed at the end of the nineteenth century, led by Andrey Markov (1856–1922).

But it was only very recently, less than a century ago, that the foundations of probability theory were laid definitively and with singular clarity by the most inconvenient of mathematicians: Someone actively involved in World War I (for the Central Powers and against the Allies) and in unmasking what would be called the subjective theory of probability. He was unfortunate, because the subjective theory had been championed by no other than John Maynard Keynes, who at the time was the most influential (and charismatic) economist. These two stain spots on his otherwise immaculate career (he would become the Gordon-McKay Professor of Aerodynamics and Applied Mathematics at Harvard University in 1944) were enough to earn him a cruel indifference towards his work on the foundations of probability theory, titled "*Probability, Statistics and Truth*", first published in 1928.

If this author had published his work before the times of the French Revolution, or if Andrey Markov had survived long enough to comment on Keynes' essay, his ideas on probability would have likely outlasted him. But history is flushed with tragic coincidences. Notwithstanding them, by 1928, he had impeccably demonstrated that:

> *…It is possible to speak about probabilities only in reference to a properly defined collective. A collective is a mass phenomenon or an unlimited sequence of observations fulfilling the following two conditions: (i)* **the relative frequencies of particular attributes within the collective tend to fixed limits** *(ii) these fixed limits are not affected by any place selection. That is to say, if we calculate the relative frequency of some attribute not in the original sequence, but in a partial set, selected according to some fixed rule, then we require that the relative frequency so calculated should tend to the same limit as it does in the original set. The fulfillment of the condition (ii) will be described as the Principle of Randomness or the Principle of the Impossibility of a Gambling System…* [6]

The first quoted sentence above, in my view, should be clear enough to conclude that in Finance, the only proper collectives we can speak of are asset classes. To demand more granularity would be inappropriate. We can think of

---

[6] Von Mises, Richard. (1928). *Probability, Statistics and Truth. Summary of the Definition, First Lecture.* Second revised English Edition, prepared by Hilda Geiringer. Mineola, NY: Dover Publications, Inc.

stocks or convertible notes or credit default swaps as collectives. And only as such, can we begin to open to the notion that we can assign probabilities to them. It is a whole other game to say that one can assign probabilities to particular stocks, or loans or swaps or portfolios. Every single one of them is a property title on (or related to, in the case of derivatives) a unique entrepreneurial undertaking. However, modern portfolio theory does not acknowledge this point. To illustrate, let me give an example: We can speak of probabilities in relation to a collective named "men aged between 25 and 35 years who drive". It is possible to observe that x% of these men have car accidents on a single day. But it is not correct to say that because I am a 30-year old man who has a car, when I drive out today, I will have an x% chance of having an accident. I am a unique individual, with unique driving skills and past driving experiences, and each accident is a particular, unique unrepeatable historical event.

As apparent as this mistaken extrapolation may seem, today, practically every financial valuation formula is predicated on this fallacy: Options, futures, credit default swaps, loans, bonds are assessed every second of every trading day using probability theory. Ratings agencies provide credit risk migration tables that are used to that end by every credit portfolio manager. However, each company subject to said valuation sells a unique product or service, in a particular market and at a particular historical time, run by unique managers. Furthermore, when banks assign capital to their loans, based on probabilities of default and expected losses, they ignore that they themselves have a significant impact on any bankruptcy process, as they can renegotiate credit terms and waive covenants, if any. And until here, I have not even addressed condition (ii) above, on randomness.

But how did we end up applying to such misleading degree the theory of probability to Finance? Very simply, it was not the theory of Finance that evolved towards the use of probability, but the theory of probability that evolved into a subjective approach, whereby collectives and frequencies themselves were no longer relevant.

In 1921[7] a British mathematician called John Maynard Keynes wrote his *Treatise on Probability*. According to him, "*...a definition is not possible, unless it contents us to define degrees of probability-relation by reference to degrees of rational belief...*" (Chapter 1, "Fundamental Ideas", section 8).

I invite the reader to compare with the previous definition offered above. This esoteric view of a branch of mathematics was also used by Keynes when he addressed capital markets: He came up with the term "animal spirits", to describe what his intelligence could not grasp.

---

[7] Andrey Markov would pass away one year later.

Under the subjective theory of probability, the mere presumption of likelihood justifies the use of probability calculus. And once this line is crossed, the rest follows, and we end up freely applying to the study of human action concepts pertaining to statistics of physics, like Markov chains and Brownian motion models, which belong to the kinetic theory of gases. But the price of a security is not comparable to a gas molecule. A security is the property title on an identified cash flow stream (potential or existing) and directly linked and determined by those who control the company that issued said securities. Whoever disputes this conclusion must explain why their models do not pass the test of randomness: Depending on the time sequence their observations belong to, the value of their variables differ. Ratings agencies sell databases on observed correlations that are updated monthly, for instance.

It is also not valid to appeal to the law of large numbers. It appears that the confusion between the subjective theory of probability and this law was originated in Poisson's book *Recherches sur la probabilité des jugements en matière criminelle et en matière civile*, published in 1837. However, Poisson was very explicit on the conditions that allow the use of probability theory. In his own words:

> ...*Les choses de toutes natures sont soumises à une loi qu'on peut appeler la loi des grands nombres. Elle consiste en ce que si l'on observe des nombres très considérables d'événements **de même nature** ...*

Indeed, Poisson suggested that things of all kinds are subject to a law that can be named the law of large numbers. But he is also clear about this law: It is based on the observation of a very considerable number of events **of a same kind**. For what matters to us, investing, I fail to see how any particular feature or behaviour of one company, reflected on its capital structure, could be observed a very considerable number of times, let alone extrapolate such observations, if available, to judge those of other companies, in different markets, times, with different products and under different management teams.

The Concept of Liquidity

The concept of liquidity is in itself complex and, like so many others within social sciences, it has mutated. With the acceptance of fractional reserve banking, the developments witnessed in money markets since the 1970s present a challenge to our personal finances.

The concept of liquidity already puzzled the minds of ancient Greek philosophers. From those times until, I dare say, sometime in the twentieth century, liquidity had been considered within a subjective context. One would have probably best referred to it as "liquidity preference", which is the term still used by John Maynard Keynes in his *General Theory*, in 1936. This preference for liquidity would have been satisfied in different degrees, according to necessity.

Perhaps one of the oldest ways to address this necessity was the adoption of bimetallism. The simultaneous use of silver and gold in different coins and weights to satisfy the liquidity preferences of a specific group does not seem to have been initiated by the regular needs of commerce, but by the tangible and pressing urge to finance armies. Alexander the Great, faced with the challenge of supplying money to his troops scattered across the Persian Empire, enforced bimetallism.[8] The same challenge met those in command of the allied troops fighting Napoleon at the beginning of the nineteenth century, and we see that until that time, liquidity preference is simply satiated with an improvement in the logistics concerning the delivery of a stable and widely accepted medium of exchange.[9]

Liquidity had always been understood within the sphere of human action. Different degrees of liquidity preference required higher or lower availability of money. But it was entirely acknowledged that only money would satisfy this preference. Throughout history, governments attempted to either debase money or enforce ratios of exchange between silver and gold or impose a par value to a commodity or accept the free circulation of foreign coins, renouncing to seigniorage. But the idea of expanding credit at an aggregate level to increase purchasing power is only characteristic of the age of democracy. Until the eighteenth century, as far as I know, it had not been considered by an absolute monarch.

In the United States, the Spanish silver dollar was accepted until the Civil War. Bimetallism was an essential feature of this country's early monetary history. But with the Revolution, things changed. The same occurred in France, where the *assignats* were enforced into circulation.

In summary, until practically the nineteenth century, it was understood that liquidity was not the intrinsic attribute of an asset, but a subjective category. Rulers always sought to address an increase in liquidity preference by

---

[8] According to Lewis Vance Cummings, the introduction of the Philippian gold stater (8.6 grams) equated in value the then familiar Persian gold daric (8.34 grams). It circulated together with the Phoenician silver stater (14.5 grams), and at the time of Alexander's conquests, the ratio of silver to gold was dropped to 10:1 from 12:1 (as a result of the increase in output from the mines of Mount Pangeum). There were other coins in circulation as well within the Macedonian Empire, and this diversity of coinage was put to use in support of mercenary forces.

[9] During the Napoleonic Wars, the successful resolution of this problem rewarded the Rothschild brothers with an epic fortune.

raising the supply of money. And they did not accomplish this by forcing the entry of new coins or new standards of value. Most times, they incorporated what had already materialized into money (through spontaneous social coordination) and they worked with it. Whenever they departed from this general discipline, Gresham's Law[10] and inflation operated their consequences without mercy.

By the latter half of the nineteenth century, there is a change in the view on liquidity. In 1874, Léon Walras writes about what he calls *"valeur d'echange"* *and* tells us that it is an attribute of goods.[11] Ironically, Carl Menger also shared this view. In his 1892 *Schriften über Geldtheorie und Währungspolitik*, Menger points to the different degrees of liquidity inherent to different goods. In his excellent explanation on the origin of money (*"Der Ursprung allgemein gebräuchlicher Tauschvermittler"*), Menger devotes a few pages to discuss how different (section 3, *Die verschiedene Gangbarkeit (Marktgängigkeit) der Güter*) degrees of liquidity (*marktgängigkeit*) proper to different goods led to the discovery of gold as the best, most useful commodity to be used as money. He is also the first to suggest that the liquidity of a good should be measured by the gap between its purchasing and selling price. However, this is quite an arbitrary definition. We have all had different experiences with a same category of goods when it comes to buying and selling it. A common example is the second-hand purchase and sale of a car: I doubt that even in the most developed markets one can conclude there is a figure to which the gap between these prices converges for a same make and year, even within a single geographic area.

It is more tangible and accurate to relate liquidity to a subjective preference. However, the idea that liquidity (*marktgängigkeit*) is an attribute associated to every good has not only survived; it has thrived. Today, whenever an economist or a politician complains that a market or an asset is illiquid, what he really laments is that the potential buyer within such market or of such asset cannot afford a purchase unless he has actual tangible savings. In other words, today, **if an asset cannot be transacted with leverage, it is said to be illiquid**. This distinction, of course, is not conscious. And it has had a relevant impact on how we think financially as well as on monetary policies, globally.

---

[10] After Sir Thomas Gresham, (c. 1519–November 21, 1579), this law states that bad money will always drive out good money. But this is a gross characterization and it is now accepted that this phenomenon had been recognized already in ancient times and by previous scholars, like Copernicus or Oresme.

[11] *"La valeur d'échange est une propriété qu'ont certaines choses de n'être pas obtenues ni cédées gratuitement"*, 5ème Leçon.

Policy makers nowadays encourage legal frameworks which fall short of a Ponzi structure,[12] because in order to maintain the illusion of liquidity in a market, said frameworks require that a continuous flow of net new credit be injected. Equally mistaken are those who allocate savings to those markets: they pay a premium (or accept lower returns) to enjoy that sense of "liquidity".

The mutation in our understanding of liquidity was born after World War I, but took a dramatic boost after 1971, when the United States ended the gold convertibility of the US dollar. When the peg was terminated, the doors were opened to a colossal expansion of credit. To this day, every time a particular market is sought by market players, lobbyists or regulators to become liquid, they establish structures where leverage is built on the underlying asset to create the illusion of ease to buy and sell. In the following pages, I describe four different variations of these structures.

Deficient Liquidity Structures

Deficient liquidity structures are popular. But it was just recently, and only by a few, that their formalization was made explicit.[13] In general, in these schemes a receiver of funds promises a rate that is not achievable but can sustain the illusion that it is, thanks to the continuous net inflow of funds.

If the receiver of funds promises to deliver rp on an amount K, but only achieves rn, there will be a gap between what was promised and achieved, equal to $(rp - rn)^*K$, over the pertinent period. Accordingly, the only way this gap can be bridged is with the addition of net inflows of funds, so that:

$$\left(\text{New deposits} - \text{Withdrawals}\right) > \left(rp - rn\right) * K$$
$$\left(\text{i.e. structure survives}\right)$$

Otherwise, if:

$$\left(\text{New deposits} - \text{Withdrawals}\right) < \left(rp - rn\right) * K$$

Then, the structure collapses.

---

[12] After Charles Ponzi, a Ponzi structure is a fraudulent operation whereby funds are borrowed at promised returns that are impossible to obtain, but nevertheless paid to the lenders using funds from new lenders. The structure survives as long as there are ever new lenders joining the operation.

[13] Marc Artzrouni, Department of Mathematics, University of Pau, April, 2009.

There are multiple variations of deficient liquidity structures that we must be aware of. In the following pages, I describe some of them.[14]

Variation No. 1: Fractional Reserve Banking

Fractional reserve banking represents a variation of a deficient liquidity structure **only at an aggregate level**. The banking system promises depositors that at all times they will have availability to their deposits, called deposits on demand. The asset being deposited is fiat money, currency.[15] In addition to this amount, depositors will earn a guaranteed interest on their deposits. However, the banking system as a whole engages in fractional reserve lending, which means that the deposits that are supposedly available on demand have been on aggregate lent multiple times over. Following today's regulatory framework (i.e. Basel III), that multiple is approximately 9×.

Fractional reserve banking dates at least back to Ancient Greece, in the fourth century BC.[16] Under fractional reserve banking, the deposit contract is de facto redefined: Deposits are only available to those who happen to withdraw the first real 1/9th[17] of the promised amounts. The rest 8/9ths will not be available, if called, which gives an aleatory nature to the deposit contract.[18] Redeemability of the deposits is only a probable event. What is not probable but certain is that under a run against the banking system, the same will collapse. This is not probable because it is deterministic: The banking system is designed precisely to not be able to honour its contracts, the promises it bounded itself to fulfil. It is not probable but certain that it will not survive in the long run. A run against fractional reserve banking is not an exogenous shock. It is 100% endogenous, since the run is caused when (and not a moment before) depositors understand they find themselves in a deficient liquidity structure. This certainty over its nature is pivotal for the existence of central banks. The survival of the banking system depends on net

---

[14] A.k.a. Ponzi schemes.

[15] But it doesn't necessarily have to be fiat money. Another variation of fractional reserve banking is the overbooking of seats by airlines. Although the purchasers of airline tickets, who reserve a seat do not have a property right on the airplane, their claim to the seat is equally aleatory and the airlines who sell them speculate on the possibility of "no-shows".

[16] However, as no central banks existed, fractional reserve banking lacked a systemic dimension.

[17] In 2016, under current global regulations.

[18] Huerta de Soto, Chapter III, *Money, Bank Credit and Economic Cycles, 3rd English Edition, 2012.*

inflows to compensate for the gap between promised and deliverable amounts. Because it is certain that such compensation eventually fails, the system is not insurable. This lack of insurability requires that, for the system to survive, an additional entity be created, which will have the legal power to enforce on depositors the exchange of liabilities from the bankrupt banks (unredeemable) for its own liabilities.

Variation No. 2: Shadow Banking

When fractional reserve banking is carried out on deposits of money, it is simply called banking. When the same fractional reserve banking is carried out on deposits of other assets also used to settle payments, it is called shadow banking. But it is politically incorrect to acknowledge this. When fractional reserve banking is practised using assets different from those that can be printed by a central bank, the problem resurfaces with an uglier face. In this case, the blame is shifted away from the system and focused on the players. The official definition of shadow banking is always a description of those who practise it, rather than of the system itself. We attack the messenger, not the message. The typical explanation is not *"Shadow banking is a practice that consists of…"*. Instead, a typical description is:

> *The shadow banking system is a term for the collection of non-bank financial inter-mediaries that provide services similar to traditional commercial banks but outside normal financial regulations.*

And with this perspective and the hands tied by the impossibility of a central bank to extend its powers beyond fiat money,[19] governments hope that with tougher regulation addressed to the sinners, the source of the sin itself will be hidden under the rug. Why is shadow banking allowed? Simply because if it is ever appropriately examined by a serious judicial enquiry, the conclusion would inevitably also reach currency banking. Any opposition to shadow banking on the grounds that a deposit should be properly considered a custody contract, rather than a loan, would have to be valid not just for shares or bonds deposited but for fiat money as well.

---

[19] Central banks cannot "print" ex nihilo shares of companies, bonds, used to collateralize lending.

Variation No. 3: Commodity ETFs

Commodity exchange-traded funds (ETFs) are so twenty-first century.[20] They raise funds by issuing units to purchase either long or short commodities futures contracts. In so doing, the retail "investor" gains clean and simple exposure to a commodity. Some ETFs offer a 2× or 3× levered exposure. Before their creation, if a retail investor[21] had wanted to have exposure to natural gas, one would have had to buy the stock of a natural gas exploration and production company. Consequently, the investor would have gained exposure not only to natural gas but also to the management of a company. It was not a pure and simple trade. Why then would ETFs be considered a variation of a deficient liquidity structure?

A deficient liquidity structure is defined by the existence of two necessary conditions: (1) The promise of a return that is higher than achievable and (2) the ability to sustain condition #1, thanks to a structure that generates positive net inflows of cash. This means that the structure attracts deposits that surpass the amounts redeemed/withdrawn at a pace that can both pay the promised return and the redemptions. Without these positive net inflows, the scheme cannot survive with the passage of time.

Because commodity ETFs are long or short a futures contract and these have a defined maturity, they must be constantly rolled over. The managers of the ETF have to "buy the roll"[22] and their counterparties know it. Probably, the cost of the roll is higher than it should be, but that is the subject of a different discussion. In any case, the profit or loss of a commodity ETF holder is formally defined as:

$$\text{Profit} = \text{Mark} - \text{to} - \text{market} - \text{magmt expenses} - \text{roll} - \text{initial investment}$$

From the equation above, it can be seen that the cost of holding a commodity ETF unit increases with time. It has a carry cost, embedded in the roll. Every month, for instance, management has to sell the expiring contract and buy a new one-month futures contract.

---

[20] An exchange-traded fund is a marketable security that may track an index (of equities or bonds or commodities) or a commodity. It trades like a common stock.

[21] A retail investor is someone who does not have the means to escape the restrictions imposed by the system he is in. He can only accept them.

[22] In a commodity futures ETF, management of the ETF has to track the "on-the-run" commodity futures contract. If this "on-the-run" contract changes every n months, at the end of the period, the ETF management is forced to sell their until-then on-the-run position, to replace it with the upcoming one. This has a cost and the sellers of those contracts, that is, the counterparties to the ETF managers, know that and are prepared to exploit it to their advantage.

Have the ETFs promised a return to the investors? Certainly not. But it is safe to assume that whatever the return an investor expects, it will always be positive. If it is not, in the long term, the cost of the roll should deplete the entire investment. This would not be odd since commodity cycles can last years and produce end prices that are multiples of the starting price. Think of oil going from $20/bbl to $120/bbl and vice versa. Any investor betting on the wrong side of the trade should lose its capital very quickly, taking the value of the respective ETF units to zero. The ETF would have to be dissolved. But this has not been the case. Whenever a commodity ETF is losing, in order to sustain its existence, management exercises reverse splits.[23] For instance, if the value of a unit falls from $1 to $0.1, they will do a 10× reverse split so that the new value is again $1. In doing so, they maintain a positive value for the units, allowing them to continue marketing investors.

In conclusion, even if an expected (although not promised) positive return is not achievable, ETFs purposely carry out reverse splits to fulfil condition #2 above: To ensure the survival of the structure by attracting funds in conjunction with reverse splits. The ETF investor that is on the losing side of the trade will still lose his capital, regardless of how much the ETF raises, but the ETF itself and the counterparties that sell the rolls will survive. This is why a commodity ETF is not a pure deficient liquidity structure, but a variation of it.

Variation No. 4: Clearinghouses (with Physical Delivery)

A clearinghouse is an institution created to diversify counterparty risk[24] by intermediating in the delivery of a bilateral contract. In so doing, the risk of contract settlements no longer depends on single counterparties, but on the collective members of the clearinghouse. However, the members' liability to the clearinghouse is limited. In addition, clearinghouses enter into contracts with banks, who provide them with financial letters of credit, to support their liquidity risk. In this sense, the risk of failure to deliver by a clearinghouse is coupled to the entire financial system, compromising central banks themselves.

---

[23] A reverse split is, as the name suggests, the act of merging again that what had been split: If an ETF had 10,000 units outstanding and marketed and decided to do a reverse split of 10:1, the result is an ETF of 1000 new units.

[24] Counterparty risk, in a contract, refers to the risk that the counterparty to it may not be able to fulfil it, regardless of the reason (usually, because the counterparty defaults).

The deficient liquidity structure variation proper to a clearinghouse of commodities futures contracts with physical delivery consists in promising said (physical) delivery but sustaining the promise with a structure that supports the monetary settlement of the delivery. This means that as long as the members of the clearinghouse accept the settlement of their contracts financially, rather than with physical delivery, the amount of outstanding traded volumes can surpass that underlying the contracts (although legally, there remains legal title to delivery). Therefore, the amount (not the return) promised for delivery is higher than the one that can be really achieved, thanks to the clearinghouse. This is a problem, because should the clearinghouse ever default on its obligation to deliver the physical commodity, creditors will have no remedy. No financial institution can print a commodity. Under these stressing circumstances, the very failure of the clearinghouse would trigger the spiralling of the commodity price. Eventually, a price for financial settlement would have to be "discovered", but in the sake of protecting the "system" from further risks, governments usually intervene and fix that price at a below market level. To the reader, this variation may seem odd, since its collapse occurs less frequently than a financial crisis. However, this is due to the fact that redeemability of commodities is prevented by regulators.[25]

High-Frequency Trading

Perhaps the fact that high-frequency trading (HFT) exists today constitutes the best proof of how far we have gone to corrupt the concept of liquidity. What is HFT? I cannot address this topic exhaustively but will only say that HFT consists in using sophisticated technology to trade securities. I will not deal here with HFT whose main task is to front-run trading orders. The HFT discussed here employs algorithms to analyse incoming market data. The associated algorithms are designed to hold investment positions very briefly only; less than a second, with HFT in and out of positions intra-day tens of thousands of times. And at the end of a trading day, there is no net investment position. Processing speed and access to the exchanges are also critical.

---

[25] While this occurs de facto, it has been established de jure in the case of credit default swaps clearing. Originally, credit default swaps could be physically cleared, by taking delivery of the defaulted obligations (i.e. bonds). But with the increase in defaults, particularly after 2007, it became evident that because the amount of credit exposure traded in credit default swaps (an unfunded contract) was multiple times that of the underlying reference bonds, physical delivery was an option that could no longer be honoured, if exercised. The credit default swap market was decoupled from the bond market.

HFT strategies can be broadly thought in terms of three main groups: Those that provide liquidity,[26] those that trade headlines and those that trade statistics.[27] The statistical ones are the easiest to understand: They are based on technical analysis. The headline strategies seek to profit from momentum trading, filtering information that describes intra-day action in the exchanges. The so-called liquidity strategies are either based on market making (to profit from bid/ask spreads) or from rebate trading. Operationally, HF traders collectively send millions of orders, the most part of which (above 90%) are cancelled before they are even hit. This often causes delays in the exchanges that receive them, potentially creating arbitrage opportunities in securities traded in multiple exchanges.[28]

Two main factors have been put forward in support of HFT:

a) **HFT provides liquidity to markets**

This point has been misunderstood, because we cannot refer to the liquidity of a particular asset but, more properly, to liquidity preference. Liquidity is not a condition intrinsic to an asset but the result of preference by market participants. For them to allocate some of their savings to liquid assets, there is no need to see millions of quotes a day, for instance, on a risky junior mining company with assets overseas, thereby creating the illusion that the junior mining equity space is liquid. In other words, market participants do not need to see the universe of liquid assets expanded to satisfy their respective liquidity preferences. And if they have to get their savings out of an asset which until a minute ago seemed liquid but now is not, they will be able to do that with or without HFT, because there is no reason to believe that under a shock, the HFT bid will not disappear in a nanosecond, making the situation even worse.

The impact of the quoting activity by HF traders distorts capital markets and particularly, the capital structure of an economic system. Companies that, given the nature of their businesses, would have been forced to raise secured long-term bank debt to fund their capital expenses before the influence of HFT may now find it easier and cheaper to raise public equity. And those market participants with investable assets captive in the system (i.e. registered

---

[26] Also known as "spoofing".

[27] Headline HF strategies are trading algorithms that react to breaking news. For instance, on May 1, 2017, upon President Trump's comment that he is "open to breaking up big banks", the value of the common stock of the big banks in the United States suffered a shock to the downside in a fraction of a second.

[28] For an enjoyable read on this subject, refer Michael Lewis' *Flash Boys*, 2014.

funds) can now fall prey to very risky projects, under the belief that they are protected by electronic stop-loss orders. Banks that might have willingly provided secured lending to these equity issuers will now find that they can only bid to them less profitable working capital lines, under the belief that their loans are protected by stock pledges. And it gets even worse: Those who invest in this equity may decide to pledge it under, say, a 3× coverage ratio[29] to borrow funds and invest in even riskier, "more compelling" assets! **The liquidity argument in favour of HFT is one more Keynesian version of the notion that inventing purchasing power ex nihilo can get us somewhere better, only this time, applied to the capital structure in particular.**

How does HFT invent purchasing power? The liquidity premium embedded in assets that wouldn't otherwise be considered "liquid" or would simply not even exist is the purchasing power we referred to. For this same reason, those who defend HFT now fear that by prohibiting it we will see a collapse in valuations.

b) HFT facilitates the process of price discovery

What media and those in favour of HFT commonly refer to price discovery is nothing else but algorithms sniffing stop losses, causing volatility in the process. There is nothing in particular about HFT with respect to pricing that humans could not achieve on their own. Throwing orders to exchanges that are immediately cancelled, to test floors or caps on the price of a certain asset, cannot be credited with price discovering. Indeed, efficient markets are those which always challenge valuations, preventing in the misallocation of resources from further expanding. But the challenge of valuations always represents the challenge of their underlying assumptions: Sales, leverage, productivity, management and so on. Shaking the nest, the way HFT does (with the sudden introduction of millions of quotes) to "discover" key levels is hardly the feature of a healthy capital market.

As an analogy, consider this: Human lives are not traded. Yet, if a criminal kidnapped somebody's daughter and asked for a ransom, he would certainly be "discovering" the price of her life: The parents of the girl, having offered all they had in immediate liquid assets, would have signalled the criminal what the price for their daughter is. Now, this is exactly what algorithms do when testing price levels in the absence of economic news, as we have painfully seen across a myriad of asset classes. Legal considerations aside, this is not a healthy

---

[29] A coverage ratio, in this context, refers to the ratio of the value of the collateral pledged to the amount borrowed. If a borrower loans $1000 under a 3.0× coverage ratio, it means that the market value of the securities pledged, collateralizing said loan, will at all times have to be at least $3000.

way to price assets, because just like the parents had never thought of trading their daughter for money, market participants not challenged by economic developments but by millions of fake orders were forced to trade too. A trade actually took place in an otherwise illiquid market but…what will happen next time? Neither the daughter will be left alone by the parents nor will our market participants be there for someone to profit from them, which is why retail money may keep flowing out of the stock exchanges (the system) as long as HFT survives.

Perhaps too, our fictional criminal will regret not having given the parents more time to liquidate more assets, but of course, that would have come at the cost of higher risk. There is no difference between the criminal's short-term line of reasoning and that which keeps HF traders from keeping positions for longer than seconds. Therefore, if we were really thinking about price discovery, neither our criminal nor HF traders did discover the true price. In the end, all we ended up with was volatility that will exponentially increase, as the savings impacted by HFT participants leave public markets.

Sovereign Risk

Sovereign risk, like the concept of liquidity, has undergone change. In essence, the change is this: Prior to the enforcement of fiat money (i.e. sovereign credit) as legal tender, sovereign risk was understood as the risk of confiscation by the sovereign. With the widespread success of the enforcement of fiat money, sovereign risk is understood today as the risk of default by the sovereign. When I refer to a sovereign, I refer to any entity that is able to enforce taxes to collect the means necessary for repayment of its obligations.

This mutation in the concept of sovereign risk took mainstream Finance practitioners to believe in three fallacies. They are based on the false comparison of a sovereign bankruptcy with that of a private debtor.

Fallacy No.1: Creditors Are Safe as Sovereigns Do Not Vanish

The first fallacy is the belief that, because a sovereign cannot physically disappear like a privately owned going concern, the creditor will be protected against the total wipe-out of his investment in sovereign debt. I will not delve into this, as territoriality is not key to understand this issue. But politics is. Indeed, for all practical purposes, Russia has always existed and will surely outlive the reader and writer. However, when it comes to testing the debt repayment capacity of this sovereign, it is noteworthy that, over a century, those in charge of honouring its sovereign debt lost their capacity to do so: From the Tsar to the Soviet Republic, and almost Putin in a few years ago. The lesson here is that if we think that purchasing sovereign debt will protect us from the vagaries of markets, we are deluding ourselves. It is precisely when we witness a wave (i.e. not just a few) of defaults in the private sector, which is always, always the exclusive outcome of previous economic interventions by the same sovereign, that its taxing and collecting abilities are most challenged and sovereign default ensues. The outcome is unfailingly a change of ruling class, regularly preceded by revolution.[30]

Fallacy No. 2: You Collect More from a Sovereign

The second fallacy is that, once in default, there will still be more left to collect from a sovereign debtor than from a private one. This is not just a belief but an imposed view, legally reflected in financial regulation. Today, under the Basel III international regulatory framework, lending institutions are allowed to set lower amounts of capital aside (in case the debtor defaults) if the debtor is a sovereign. The so-called loss-given-default capital factor of a sovereign is lower than that assigned to a private borrower. Nothing could be farther from reality. Simply imagine yourself trying to enforce collection from the federal government of Argentina, instead of a global corporate or even the Argentinean subsidiary of a global corporate. Just the difference in legal costs would be overwhelming. However, the standard official optic on this point is that you are safer financing the sovereign (who has policing and taxing power over you) than financing your neighbour. In the words of the Basel Committee on Banking Supervision (Chapter 5 of their 2001 Consultative Document):

> *The Committee's work indicated that banks' assessment of loss severity or LGD[31] for sovereign exposures is not well developed. The evaluation of LGD is difficult due to scarce loan recovery data. Some banks have tried to estimate loss severity by measuring the economic loss experienced by defaulted sovereign bondholders. However, this approach implicitly assumes that a sovereign defaults as frequently on both loans and bonds and negotiates equivalent recovery terms on both types of credit facilities. For*

---

[30] This has been so since times immemorial, regardless of culture or geography: In Ancient Rome, in Byzantium, Ptolemaic Egypt, Plantagenet's England, in France under Louis XVI, and most recently in the multiple sovereign defaults that took place in the twentieth century. Rulers changed and the capacity or willingness to tax in order to honour the obligations left by predecessors was nowhere evident.

[31] LGD is an acronym for "loss given default".

*a number of reasons, this assumption may not be accurate. The transparency of recovery negotiations on publicly held debt compared to bank loans may translate into **a higher recovery rate on bonds**. Sovereigns' desire to re-enter the public debt market may also strengthen the hand of bondholders in re-negotiating favourable repayment terms compared to banks.*[32]

I agree with the last statement, but we must remember that sovereign debt in the age of democracy is mostly unsecured. Before the age of democracy, rulers pledged concrete assets or taxing rights, which in my view is fairer not only to the creditors but also to the future generations of subjects (or taxpayers). When debt is unsecured, repayment is sought from future generations, and they may vote repudiation. This may very well be the trigger of the next political revolution, once today's millennials take over.

One last observation here: If one believes indeed in this fallacy, namely that the loss given default of a sovereign is of a different "nature" than that of a corporation, then the addition of the risk-free return and a beta-adjusted return to obtain an asset return would be incorrect. It violates the rule of addition of probabilities.[33]

Fallacy No. 3: Sovereign Debt in Local Currency Cannot Default

The third and most modern of all fallacies is the direct result of the ascent of fiat money. Before the age of democracy and in the absence of fiat money, rulers could only exert inflation through debasement. Debasement is an act of physical violence on money. Coins were of either lower quality or lower weight. The creditor of a sovereign could disregard any impact on prices and understand and verify the simple fact that if the sovereign paid its debt with newly minted coins of lower quality or weight, he was being expropriated. The extent of the expropriation was very tangible and there was no doubt that it amounted to one of the events that even today is technically considered to constitute default:

"A default is considered to have occurred with regard to a particular obligor when one or more of the following events has taken place:

---

[32] Refer: http://www.bis.org/publ/bcbsca05.pdf

[33] *"…Only such probabilities can be added as are attached to different attributes **in one and the same collective…**" ref.* Probability, Statistics and Truth. More on this in the next section, on Correlation.

(b) A credit loss event associated with any obligation of the obligor, such as a charge-off..." (Idem, Proposed Reference Definition of a Default Event for the IRB Framework)

As this is a book about Finance, I will not examine the causes that conceded sovereigns all over the world the ability to gradually escape the rigour of commodity money, to enjoy the comfort of fiat money. However, Prof. Miguel Anxo Bastos has very succinctly explained this[34]: When political power is fragile, and no single sovereign can easily project it beyond the borders of his dominions, he is by necessity wary of incurring into debts. Until recently, rulers had to secure their possessions with mercenary forces and only pure, unquestionable gold could afford them. This was most painfully true for the Spanish Taifas or the allied forces fighting Napoleon. And vice versa: the first rulers that were able to project their power unchallenged over a vast geography were the ones who were able to first impose fiat money on their subjects, beginning with the Great Khan.

The third fallacy thus consists in concluding that because a sovereign can impose fiat money as legal tender, it can never default, for the full amount owed will always be repaid in said fiat money. Yesterday, the central bank needed only to print new currency to refinance the debt owed. Today, all it takes to repay a debt is a digital accounting entry between the sovereign's treasury and the central bank. If this were true, there would be no need to issue sovereign debt to begin with (although as we will see later, there are those who think that the ultimate goal of issuing sovereign debt is to set a positive rate of interest).[35] Ignoring for a moment if debt paid in depreciated currency constitutes an act of default, for all practical purposes the fact is that to the sovereign bondholder, purchasing power has undoubtedly been expropriated. This is all what counts. **If this judgement was erred, private debts could be settled with assets different than originally contracted, regardless of their different values.**

The experience of Argentina's central bank in 2016 is illustrative. To bring inflation down, this central bank issues notes in pesos. In April of 2016, these notes paid 38%. The goal of the central bank is to attract enough buyers, to maintain their pesos out of the banking system (Fig. 1.1).

As you can see from the chart below, the central bank was losing the game (Fig. 1.2).

---

[34] Miguel Anxo Bastos (Universidad Santiago de Compostela), *Política Exterior Liberal*, presentation at the X Universidad de Verano, Instituto Juan de Mariana, Lanzarote, July, 2105: https://youtu.be/Zt7CfsNh3EQ?t=24m43s

[35] This view is held by what is currently known as Modern Monetary Theory.

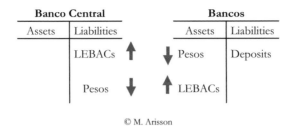

© M. Arisson

Fig. 1.1 Consolidated balance sheets of the Banco Central and Argentina's banking system

Banco Central de la República Argentina: Yield curve on April 14, 2016

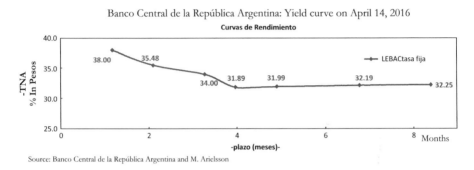

Source: Banco Central de la República Argentina and M. Arielsson

Fig. 1.2 Yield curve of the Banco Central de la República Argentina: April 14, 2016

The yield curve for their *peso* liabilities was inverted. In any other case within the corporate debt space, a yield curve like this represents imminent default.[36] The 38% upfront in the curve would mean in a high-yield market that the credit trades at recovery values. In this case, where the amount owned is actually printed by the central bank (which is the basis for the third fallacy), the default is also imminent and it means the total wipe-out of the peso as a currency. The 38% upfront simply implies that the market expects hyperinflation to take place within two to three years (i.e. 100%/38%). This is living proof that default is possible even when a sovereign has to pay back with its own currency. The default, of course, is of a different nature, because the value of said currency evaporates.

However, in spite of the three fallacies just described, financial institutions today are allowed to attribute no risk weight to the lending they extend to sovereign borrowers. This is nothing short than legalized discrimination

---

[36] When the short end of a credit curve is at a higher level than the long end, pushing the intertemporal exchange rate of said credit to a negative slope, the curve signals a near-term risks of default. Inverted credit curves mean that near-term bond coupons are more risky than implied by flat or steep curves.

against any entrepreneur who seeks financing for his projects. For the direct or indirect (i.e. those who finance sovereign debt with their bank deposits, unknowingly) creditors, the risk of their investment is systematically downplayed.

Correlation (or Modern Portfolio Theory)

According to the Encyclopaedia Britannica, a tautology, in Logics, is "...*a statement so framed that it cannot be denied without inconsistency....*" A tautology is a phrase or expression in which the same thing is said twice in different words.

In this regard, one can't but notice that, over the past decades, we have slowly come to believe that securities are stochastic[37] elements and seem to have forgotten that instead they are a property title on an entrepreneurial venture. Modern finance practitioners today think of returns on securities in terms of a function, where one of the parameters is called "beta":

$$R\,a, t = a + b \times r \text{ benchmark}, t + \mathrm{e}t$$

In the equation above, we see that the return of an asset "*a*" depends on that of its benchmark market, adjusted by beta. The return of asset *a* can thus be estimated from a regression,[38] where Beta is:

$$\beta = \frac{\mathrm{Cov}\left(r_a, r_b\right)}{\mathrm{Var}\left(r_b\right)}$$

Beta, Therefore, Is a Tautology Entrepreneurial activity is not stochastic and one cannot extrapolate future returns based on past experience. It is not true that securities came to be ex nihilo or that individual expected returns show a converging relative frequency that simultaneously passes a test of randomness and whose probability can be calculated. When we "calculate" said probability, we make the gross mistake of allowing ourselves to believe that the security represents another physical, inanimate object. This tautology has a tangible impact on how we invest.

---

[37] Within a Brownian motion stochastic process.

[38] Regression analysis is a method in statistics used to estimate relationships between variables. For the inquisitive reader, there is Damodar Gujarati's 2009 *Essentials of Econometrics*.

As an outcome of this mental tool called Beta, we have developed index funds that seek to optimize "diversification".[39] But did we not think diversification was necessary in the past? How did we come to look and even pay a premium or management fees for diversification?[40] The development of public markets is at the core of this question, as well as the beginning of collective (and coercive) savings plans.[41] The allocation of centrally enforced (and often centrally planned) savings required efforts of such scale that the universe of private, granular and diversified investments offered at the beginning of the twentieth century could not assist with. It was imperative to create a legal framework where investments in public markets could compete on an (illusory) equal foot with private ones, like the real estate market. And thus, after centuries of slow but steady developments in financial markets, three major breakthroughs were imposed: the development of limited liability, the prohibition of insider trading and the encouragement of deficient liquidity structures that create the illusion of liquidity in public markets. I have written about the latter in the previous pages. I write about the first two legal developments in Lesson 4.

Diversification is definitely not new. In fact, there is a strong case to believe that fractional reserve banking was motivated by the desire to diversify. Indeed, bankers did not feel safeguarding their clients' deposits (in gold coins). They were an easy loot[42] for their own or for foreign monarchs. But the concept of Beta, embedded in modern portfolio theory, is not just about

---

[39] Portfolio diversification is a process or technique consisting in selecting securities whose correlation, with the portfolio, diminishes to an "optimal" level, the volatility of the portfolio. In other words, it is another tautological exercise.

[40] The premium consists in accepting lower returns in exchange for diversification or less volatility of a portfolio of securities.

[41] The first pension fund was created in Prussia, under Otto Von Bismarck. Pension contributions are a tax, actually: Citizens of Prussia were coerced to save, to fund a universal pension that would kick in at the age of 65, at a time when the average life expectancy was below 65.

[42] The monetary history of the Spanish colonies in America is nothing short of a list of confiscations. These were truly humiliating, for the gold holdings seized were sent to Spain for appraisal, to examine their purity, at the expense of those confiscated. The appraisals could last years. When the seized gold had finally been assessed, the merchants were paid with bonds (called "juros"), paying below market yields. The first such confiscation took place in Mexico, through the Casa de Contratación, according to the Oficio IV, 9152, folio 290, on January 17, 1525. The unlucky merchant was a certain Don San Juan de Ojirondo, born in Vergara. Sixteen months later, Ojirondo hired a former neighbour, Don Nicolás Sánchez de Aramburu and a friend at the Court, Don Martín de Vergara, to represent his case before the king and obtain the release of said "juros". Even the same Pizarro brothers, who brought so much wealth and glory to the Spanish crown, were confiscated in 1536. Their wealth was exchanged for "perpetual" juros: They never recovered the principal, but enjoyed an annual yield of 3.3% on it, as determined by the king. See Sardone, Sergio "*Los secuestros de las remesas americanas de particulares de Carlos V a través de los notarios sevillanos*", *Temas Americanistas, Número 29, 2012, pp. 21–64.*

diversification. **Implicit in it is also the idea that the performance**[43] **of a security is not all related to that of the issuer** (i.e. the management of the issuing company), but instead consists of a core part, the so-called risk-free return, and another, the return produced by the issuer, adjusted precisely by Beta. The whole construction, once again, is a tautology.

Beta, as a stochastic parameter, can be applied to any security. But it is mostly used to estimate equity and debt returns. When Beta is used to explain the return of a stock, it does so in terms of its correlation with a relevant equity market. Without examining what is understood by a (public) equity market or what particular benchmark is chosen for that matter, implicit in this formulation, is **the assumption of the existence of a relative frequency of volatility in equity returns**. If we remember what a relative frequency is, we realize that extrapolating it to the uncertainties of a managerial venture makes no sense. The idea of a relative frequency of volatility demands that there be a mean return when all one can state about equity is only valid when equity is considered as a collective, as an asset class: That its return converges to a non-negative number. Modern portfolio theory therefore ignores entrepreneurship (and monetary policy[44]) as deterministic, because it plays no role in determining the return of equity.

When beta is applied to credit portfolios, the underlying assumptions get even less realistic:

$$R\,a = \text{risk} - \text{free rate}\left(\text{sovereign risk}\right) + b\,\text{risk premium}\,a$$

In addition to the above objections, the use of beta in credit consists in the addition of two probabilities that have nothing in common, because they do not belong to the same collective: The probability of default by the sovereign (i.e. sovereign risk) and the probability of default by the corporate (risk premium *a*), whose credit return is being valued. Once more, this point was addressed in *Probability, Statistics and Truth*:

...Perhaps some of you will remember from school days references to the probability of "either-or" and the following proposition concerning the calculation of unknown probabilities from known ones: The probability of casting either 2 or 4 or 6 is equal to the sum of the probabilities of each of these results separately. This statement is, however, inexact; it remains incomplete even if we say that only probabilities of mutually exclusive events can be added in this way. The probability of dying in the

---

[43] Here again, performance denotes a mechanistic view.
[44] For a discussion on monetary policy and systemic risk, see Lesson 7: "Systemic Risk".

interval between one's fortieth and the forty-first birthday is, say, 0.011, and that of marrying between the forty-first and the forty-second birthday is 0.009. The two events are mutually exclusive; nevertheless we cannot say that a man entering his forty-first year has the chance 0.011+0.009 = 0.020 of either dying in the course of this year or marrying in the course of the following year.

*The clarification and the ensuing correct formulation of the mixing operation can only be achieved by having recourse to the concept of the collective. The difference between the correct formulation of the addition rule and the incorrect one follows from the principle that only such probabilities can be added as are attached to different attributes **in one and the same collective**...*[45]

The fundamental causes and dynamics of corporate and sovereign defaults are different, and it is self-evident that they do not form part of a same collective. Given the explanation above, the addition of these two probabilities of default (i.e. risks), even if they existed as such, constitute an abuse and a misunderstanding of the theory of probability.

Conclusion

We have discussed the tools, underlying ideas and context in which mainstream Finance works today. They all find their source in political events and concepts that took place at the end of the eighteenth century.

Because ideas drive facts (and not the other way around), we began examining the former. Three main dogmas dominate Modern Finance. They are dogmas because they are not to be challenged, but simply accepted, because everyone else accepts them. But they are not institutions. They did not come into existence from popular and spontaneous cooperation. These are the following:

- The belief in continuity in human action
- The belief in a natural state of equilibrium
- The acceptance of subjective assessments as grounds for use of probability theory

The facts that sprang from these ideas are so embedded in our daily routines that we can barely imagine that they once too were extreme, rather than normal. The limitation of rights to one's property under deposit (i.e. fractional reserve banking), coercive savings plans, managed intertemporal

---

[45] Second Lecture: "The Elements of the Theory of Probability, Inexact statement of the addition rule", 2nd revised edition, Dover Publications, Inc., New York.

exchange rates (also known as benchmark interest rates), the absence of sound liquidity (i.e. not credit or high-frequency spoofing) are all a reality that follows our daily attempts at not just increasing but also protecting our wealth. They are an obstacle to accomplish our basic material goals if we do not know how to handle them. The following pages are precisely an attempt to furnish the reader with the fundamentals, the theory and the practical means to do just that: To handle the multiple obstacles described in this first part of the book, which constitute the current paradigm we are immersed in.

Appendix

Aesthetics in Infinitesimal Analysis

There is a final aspect of the assumption of continuity in Finance and it is aesthetic. Aesthetics plays a defining role in human behaviour and the Theory of Finance is no exception. Under continuity, compound interest can be expressed as:

$$e^{rt}$$

Since logarithmic functions are monotonic,[46] the logarithmic transformation of compound interest comes in handy for regression analysis and results in:

$$\ln\left(e^{rt}\right) = r * t$$

One of the many examples that illustrates this aesthetic use of continuous functions in Finance is the Stochastic Portfolio Theory. In their 2008 paper, "Stochastic Portfolio Theory: An Overview", Fernholz and Karatzas begin with this basic financial market model:

$$dB(t) = B(t)r(t)\,dt, B(0) = 1$$

The equation above describes a money-market $B(\cdot)$ and stocks, whose prices are driven following a Brownian motion process and a "flow of information" F, where:

---

[46] A function is monotonic if its first derivative does not change sign.

$$F = \{F(t)\}\, 0 \le t < \infty$$

Could also be a "filtration" process generated by Brownian motion. Whoever relies a financial analysis on such a model is making the assumption one can earn a return without any jumps, continually, throughout time, and apparently at no cost. The other assumptions, at least, are consistent, because if one is to believe that stocks, which are the legal title to the cash flows produced by real companies, behave completely in a random way, one has to believe too that the information regarding such a market environment is given randomly too and at no cost. This is of course the farthest from reality one can remove oneself, because it is precisely the complete absence of cost-free information and the necessity to produce it or to discover it (in other words, the negation of all the above assumptions) what makes the essence of the entrepreneurial activity and, by transitivity, is reflected in the price of the securities that represent a title on it, namely, stocks. In other words, if economic information was free and its production was random, there would be no need for entrepreneurs or for property titles on their achievements. There would be no need for securities. How any of these portfolio theories have resisted the test of time and experience escapes me. They are however the intellectual foundation for the management of collective pools of savings.

Aesthetics in General Equilibrium Theory

The history of science is full of cases where aesthetics or a singular ideal of beauty played an important role. In Ancient Greece, philosophers were attracted to ideal shapes. In Astronomy, the beauty of the circle led astronomers to believe in circular orbits, which blinded this science until Kepler rediscovered the math behind elliptical orbits. In Economics and Finance, static analysis and the ideal of general equilibrium represent one of such cases, and are well alive to this date.[47] In the words of Fritz Machlup:

> [W]e may define equilibrium, in economic analysis, as a constellation of selected interrelated variables so adjusted to one another that no inherent tendency to change prevails in the model which they constitute.

---

[47] To the reader interested in an in-depth discussion of these terms, I recommend Fritz Machlup's *Essays on Economic Semantics* (1963).

Equilibrium analysis is an intellectual exercise of dubious utility. To begin, if "*no inherent tendency to change prevails*" in equilibrium, any Finance practitioner using general equilibrium models is simply ignoring the omnipresent feature that drives value: Change. Also, if time exists (under dynamic equilibrium models), it has a physical not an economic dimension. In this sense, variables within a dynamic equilibrium model are "predestined", and therefore, no further knowledge is gained by solving dynamic equations.[48] For instance, take the equation:

$$Y = x^* t + 1$$

Where t is the time variable within the group of whole numbers (i.e. 0, 1, 2...n)

The triplet (1, 2, 3) for (x, t, y) belongs to the group of infinite solutions for this equation, as 1*2+1 = 3. But the triplet (30, 2, 61) also belongs to the universe of possible solutions. The triplet (30, 2, 61) or (35, 3, 106) is already "predestined"; they are simultaneously implied in the equation and are no more valid than the triplet (1, 2, 3). Yet, when in dynamic equilibrium models the t variable is attributed to time, it is believed that further insight can be gained by solving it. This is particularly so in the field of valuation of securities. Equity research analysts, with their dynamic models and respective assumptions, want to project the image of a method, a science that stands out for adding value by discovering where capital is misallocated and constitutes an investment opportunity. But this is an illusion.

What made general equilibrium models so attractive and popular? Firstly, from an analytical perspective, the models allow for optimal states. Every ambitious politician that believes in central planning loves the idea of "optimizing" to make our society more efficient (according to their own criteria, of course). Secondly, general equilibrium models can be run using simple algebra. They are comfortable to work with.

Between 1874 and 1877, the works of Léon Walras surfaced the idea of general equilibrium in Economics. In 1874, Walras published *Éléments d'économie politique pure, ou théorie de la richesse sociale*, while he taught in Lausanne. His work examined the conditions necessary to reach equilibrium in an economic system, based on a system of simultaneous equations. As this is a book about Finance, not Economics, I cannot be exhaustive and therefore fair to M. Walras.

---

[48] Huerta De Soto, *Socialism, Economic Calculation and Entrepreneurship, 1992.*

Plainly speaking, it is understood that a market x is in equilibrium when there is neither an excess of supply or demand.

$$Sx - Dx = 0 \left(\text{i.e. Supply of } x - \text{Demand of } x\right) = 0$$

General equilibrium in an economic system with $(n+1)$ markets implies that if the first n markets are in equilibrium, the last market, $n+1$, must be in equilibrium as well. Suppose that there were only three markets: If two of them are in equilibrium, the third (i.e. last) will also have to be in equilibrium. Formally:

$$\left(Sx - Dx\right) + \left(Sy - Dy\right) + \left(Sz - Dz\right) = 0$$

If $Sx - Dx = 0$ (market x is in equilibrium), and $Sy - Dy = 0$, then:

$$Sz - Dz = 0$$

This conclusion is known as the Walras' Law and it goes to show that it is not necessary that all markets be balanced (i.e. in equilibrium). Only in the particular case of the Walras' Law, where the n markets show no excess of either demand or supply, will the last one, market $(n+1)$, be balanced too.

There are relevant conceptual errors derived from using general equilibrium models. This mechanistic view demands that we ignore the role of entrepreneurship, precisely when entrepreneurs are the engine behind markets. It also assumes that markets are given and static entities. And it leaves no room to include a theory of prices. To the mainstream Finance practitioner, markets can be described as mathematical finite spaces. But markets are coordination processes. It is entrepreneurs who do the coordination, and in so doing, they develop markets. As I discuss later, it is the entrepreneurs who create, who issue equity or debt and thereby choose a particular capital structure with unique voting control features, design their marketing strategies, take risks and, last but not least, have insider information that the outsider investor doesn't. Once more, the proof that the idea of equilibrium is foreign to the market process is that the relentless changes effected by entrepreneurs and consumers (every individual is simultaneously a consumer and an entrepreneur) in their selection of means and ends require that we use an institution, that is, money. In a world of general equilibrium and continuity, there is no place for money and barter should be more efficient.

A Word on Indeterminacy

The idea of a general equilibrium brings the implicit recognition of the possibility of indetermination. General equilibrium is formally addressed through equations, whereby the interrelation of variables (as defined by Fritz Machlup above) is exposed. When one isolates a group of equations relevant to the problem examined, one speaks of a system of equations. In algebra, a system is indeterminate if there is more than one solution to it. For ease, let's think of a one-equation system, where:

$$y = x + 4$$

For the equation above, the number of solutions is infinite. We cannot say that the pair (2; 6) is more valid than (4; 8) to describe the system.

In 1949, economist Don Patinkin published a work titled *The Indeterminacy of Absolute Prices in Classical Economic Theory.*[49] Patinkin decisively demonstrated that under the Walrasian analysis, the absolute level of prices cannot be determined and that markets clear (i.e. supply meets demand) thanks to relative (not absolute) prices. In other words, in the Walrasian analysis, so rooted in today's mainstream financial models, it is conceivable that multiple solutions solve a system formed by:

$$(S1 - D1), (S2 - D1), (S3 - D3).....(Sn - Dn)$$

But if indeterminate systems are conceivable from a mathematical point of view, indeterminate markets make no sense from an economic standpoint. However, the idea of indetermination is at the core of many contemporary events, like currency wars and currency coordination by central banks, or the use of structured finance products.

In the case of coordination among central banks, the system (USDCAD = 1.45, USDEUR = 1.09, USDJPY = 120…USDCHF= 1.0) is as valid and conceivable as (USDCAD = 1.25, USDEUR = 1.14, USDJPY = 125…. USDCHF = 0.90), for instance. To most institutional investors, it is as valid to purchase gold certificates as it is to buy physical gold. The same can be said for those who buy an equity tranche in a structured vehicle, rather than comparable direct equity ownership in its underlying units. This indifference between economic reality and mathematic theory can only last as long as any

---

[49] *Econometrica*, Vol. 17, No. 1 (Jan., 1949), pp. 1–27.

hint of a physical, non-virtual, insurmountable obstacle is successfully removed from the system. One such hint is the gold market. Because its supply cannot be "printed", the system:

$$(S\text{gold} - D\text{gold})$$

Remains outside the reach of central bankers. But in time, they learned to cope with this limitation, as I explain later.[50] They have done so by eliminating the redeemability of gold (from central banks) and allowing the ratio of paper to physical gold to escalate to unimaginable levels. The Walrasian analysis is the formal pillar on which a system where the inventory of paper gold is multiple times that of physical gold is sustainable.

Bibliography

Russell, Bertrand. (1922). *The Problem of China*. London. George Allen & Unwin Ltd.

Li, Chi. (1922). *Some Anthropological Problems of China*. Baltimore: Chinese Students' Monthly. Page 327

Marshall, Alfred. (1890). *Principles of Economics*. London: Palgrave Classics in Economics, Eighth Edition.

Hull, John. (1996). *Options, Futures, and Other Derivatives*. Third Edition. Upper Saddle River, NJ: Prentice Hall.

Gaxotte, Pierre. (1970). *La Révolution Française*. Paris: Éditions Tallandier, 2014.

Huerta de Soto, Jesús. (2014). *Ensayos de Economía Política*. Madrid: Unión Editorial.

Huerta de Soto, Jesús. (2008). *The Austrian School: Market Order and Entrepreneurial Creativity*. Cheltenham, UK: Edward Elgar Publishing Ltd.

Ferguson, Niall. (2008). The Ascent of Money. New York, NY: The Penguin Press.

Cummings, Lewis Vance. (1940). *Alexander The Great*. New York, NY: Grove Press, 1968.

Walras, Léon. (1926). *Éléments d'Économie Politique Pure ou Théorie de la Richesse Sociale*. Edition définitive revue et augmentée par l'auteur. Paris : H. Pichon et R. Durand –Auzias Éditeurs.

Menger, Carl. (1892 – 1909). Collected Works of Carl Menger (in German). Volume IV. London: London School of Economics and Political Science, 1936. Retrieved August, 2015, from: https://mises-media.s3.amazonaws.com/Collected%20Works%20of%20 Carl%20Menger%20%28in%20German%29%20Volume%20IV_5. pdf?file=1&type=document

---

[50] Ref. Lesson 6 "Institutions", section "Gold".

Shafer, Glenn. (1996). The Significance of Jacob Bernoulli's Ars Conjectandi for the Philosophy of Probability Today. *Journal of Econometrics*. vol. 75, issue 1, 15–32.

Bernoulli, Jakob. (1713). *Ars Conjectandi. Pars Quarta tradens Usum & Applicationem Praecedentis Doctrinae in Civilibus, Moralibues & Oeconomicis.* Translated into English by Oskar Cheinine, Berlin 2005. Retrieved September, 2015, from http://www.sheynin.de/download/bernoulli.pdf

Gaarder Haug, Espen & Taleb, Nassim N. (2010*). Option traders use (very) sophisticated heuristics, never the Black-Scholes-Merton formula. Journal of Economic Behavior & Organization*. Volume 77, Issue 2, February 2011, Pages 97–106.

Fernholz, Robert & Karatzas, Ioannis. (2008). *Stochastic Portfolio Theory: an Overview.* Retrieved September 2015, from http://www.math.columbia.edu/~ik/FernKarSPT.pdf

Hoppe, Hans-Hermann. (Spring 2007). The Limits of Numerical Probability: Frank H. Knight and Ludwig Von Mises and the Frequency Interpretation. *The Quarterly Journal of Austrian Economics*. Vol. 10, No. 1: 3–21. Retrieved September 2015, from https://mises-media.s3.amazonaws.com/qjae10_1_1.pdf?file=1&type=document

Landro, Alberto. (2010a). Acerca del "Regellosigkeitsaxiom" de Von Mises. *Cuadernos del CIMBAGE* Nro. 12: 1–21. Retrieved September 2015, from http://ojs.econ.uba.ar/ojs/index.php/CIMBAGE/article/view/351/640

Landro, Alberto. (2010b).Acerca de la existencia del verdadero valor de una probabilidad. *Revista de Economía Política de Buenos Aires*. Año 4, Vols. 7 y 8: 221–245. Retrieved September 2015, from http://ojs.econ.uba.ar/ojs/index.php/REPBA/article/view/258/464

Artzrouni, Marc. (2009). *The Mathematics of Ponzi Schemes*. Dept. of Mathematics, University of Pau. Retrieved October 2015 from: https://mpra.ub.uni-muenchen.de/14420/1/

Lewis, Michael. (2014). *Flash Boys*. New York: W.W. Norton & Company Ltd.

Basel Committee on Banking Supervision. (May 31, 2001). Operational Risk Consultative Document. Ch. V. Retrieved May, 2015 from: https://www.fsa.go.jp/inter/bis/bj_20010117_1/1n.pdf

Bastos Boubeta, Miguel Anxo. (July 2015). *Política Exterior Liberal*. Presentation at the X Universidad de Verano, Instituto Juan de Mariana, Lanzarote. Retrieved October 2015 from: https://youtu.be/Zt7CfsNh3EQ?t=24m43s

Von Mises, Richard. (1928). *Probability, Statistics and Truth*. Second revised English Edition, prepared by Hilda Geiringer. Mineola, NY: Dover Publications, Inc. Second revised English Edition, 1981.

Sardone, Sergio. (2012). Los secuestros de las remesas americanas de particulares de Carlos V a través de los notarios sevillanos. *Temas Americanistas*, Número 29, pp. 21–64.

Part II

Fundamentals

2

Asset Allocation Is Intertemporal Preference

Intertemporal Preference

Some economists will agree with the view that an interest rate is a subjective intertemporal exchange rate (between present and future consumption). Figure 2.1 illustrates the concept.

This was not always the case in the past, and for this reason, innocent people suffered persecution. In the beginning, the persecution was religious because charging (loan) interest was sinful. Later, it became political.[1] However, even though interest rates are now accepted as simple intertemporal exchange ratios, it is still common to see a mechanistic perspective associated to them. The simplest mechanistic view is that which attaches interest rates a passive role. According to it, interest rates are not subjective intertemporal ratios but are determined by the (average) marginal productivity of capital. And those within the Modern Monetary School go even farther: Interest rates are simply prices set by central banks. The current paradigm is based on these two latter perspectives, and they are implicit in what came to be known as efficient frontiers or optimal portfolios of securities (see Fig. 2.2).

Note that cash, in other words, liquidity, can be part of the optimal portfolio. But why should there be an optimal interest rate or diversified securities portfolio if the intertemporal preference is precisely a preference, a subjective preference?

---

[1] Because debtors, who also have a vote, are usually more numerous than creditors.

© The Author(s) 2018
M. Arisson, *Investing in the Age of Democracy*,
https://doi.org/10.1007/978-3-319-95903-0_2

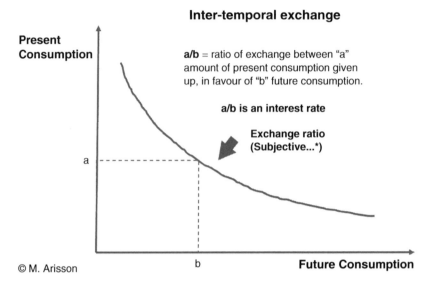

(*) Even this representation is wrong. Individuals do not decide their exchange ratio ex-ante, but only at specific times, under specific circumstances, which make the representation a simple visual tool.

Fig. 2.1 Intertemporal preference

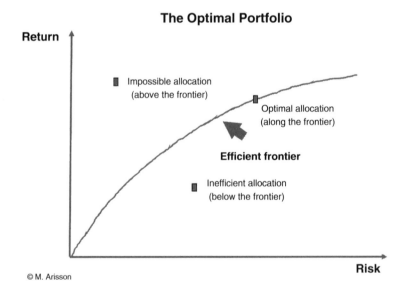

Fig. 2.2 The optimal portfolio allocation

In the "modern" mean-variance portfolio theory, the rates of returns on assets are assumed to be random variables. The optimal securities portfolio is one whose portfolio-weighting factors are optimal.

According to Markowitz,[2] the optimal set of weights is the one that obtains a target expected rate of return with minimal volatility. The optimization exercise is therefore not about intertemporal preference but about returns or yields. It represents the mechanistic perspective I referred to before, trumping any subjective consideration.

However, saving and investing are activities which, like any other, require practice to perfect and are continuously evolving. Intertemporal preference is their cornerstone, and demographic factors, like life expectancy, have a strong indirect influence on them. Reflecting upon interest rates in a mechanistic way removes us from reality, and it is in no way efficient. But this shift from a subjective and teleological point was not whimsical. It appears to me that it took place and was encouraged by the rise of democracy. Democratic regimes are based on the rule of the majority (and the subjection of minorities). When there is economic freedom, there is no conflict. But economic freedom was gradually lost during the twentieth century, as restrictions unfolded in varying degrees and at varying speeds. In the developed world, they have taken place so smoothly and slowly over generations that it is difficult to realize. In the twenty-first century, couples that manage to earn an income to sustain their families within what is commonly considered "middle class" pay their governments between 35% and 50% of what they earn.[3] Parents barely have a surplus to save and feel grateful that governments take their children under the wing of public education, while they both go to work to collect the other 50% to 65% of their earnings that is allowed them to enjoy. Only in 2016 in Canada, the amount to save free of capital gain taxes was reduced from C$10,000 per year per person to C$5500. Their savings have little room to be allocated freely, as sovereign liabilities and public markets are subsidized with biased legislation (with regard to either taxes or quotas, i.e. registered funds). There are pension plans at federal or state or municipal levels and employers are coerced to save on behalf of their employees. Investments in government liabilities (at different levels—federal, state and municipal) benefit from a tax-free treatment, and if we are still left with anything to save and allocate it in the system via registered accounts, we may receive some tax refunds. (Loan) interest rates are set by central bankers and the banking system is completely

---

[2] Harry Markowitz: "Portfolio Selection" in *The Journal of Finance* Vol. 7, No. 1 (Mar., 1952).

[3] Perhaps the only way to help visualize how enslaving the current system is would be to simply transfer the power of paying salaries to workers from employers to a government agency. The government agency would then manage a general payroll ledger on behalf of employers, issuing the payment cheques, net of income taxes.

regulated. Worldwide, the banking system also fell victim to the taxing infrastructure, as governments imposed banks to reveal transactions of their customers.

As this situation has developed already for decades, it is not surprising to see that we have lost the ancestral knowledge, transmitted from generation to generation, on how to save and invest. These are skills that have been slowly taken away from us. Popular wisdom says that they are simply influenced by interest rates and, should these rise, so will (rise) saving and investing volumes. But I disagree. It is not so simple. Saving and investing demand that we understand our intertemporal preferences, our liquidity needs, the macroeconomic context we live in, the institutions associated with these activities and so on. And we have simply lost that wealth of knowledge and instead follow regulations. This book seeks to revitalize this ancestral knowledge.

The current portfolio optimization paradigm belongs to the coercive infrastructure described above. It would not survive under free, sound money, 100% reserve banking, and no interventions in the capital markets or coercion on savings. Ontologically, it serves those who manage savings pools, to benchmark (and remunerate) their work. But optimization analysis assumes the absence of signals, of prices, of intertemporal preference. The idea of optimal diversification assumes a priori knowledge of expected returns, and these expected returns are in no way epistemologically tied to the intrinsic business potential of the securities that represent them.

In a free world, the entrepreneurial profits tend to disappear, due to competition among entrepreneurs and gross profits, on aggregate, converge to the market interest rate.[4] Because we cannot forecast who will lose or win, diversification allows investors to approach that market interest rate. This is consistent with probability theory applied to collectives like "equity" and "debt": We know that the difference between the returns shown by these two classes, over time, will show a convergence to a non-negative number.

In the current paradigm, on the other hand, expected returns are the outcome of volatilities modelled after random processes. Nothing could be further from reality. Nothing is less scientific than portfolio optimization. If we could (and we should) remove ourselves from the established paradigm, rather than think in terms of optimization, we should take the following first steps to manage our savings.

---

[4] Huerta de Soto, Chap. 4, Section 5, *Market Order and Entrepreneurial Creativity*, 2008.

1. Set your (subjective) liquidity preference

Your liquidity preference is the amount of money you (or your family) may temporarily need in case of an unexpected emergency, loss of income and more until things go back to normal again. To some, it may be the equivalent of six months of income. It can also be a certain amount you may want to hold in cash, to take advantage of a purchasing opportunity. One may target to reach this amount over a certain period. Every year you save a bit to leave liquidity towards this "emergency" fund and leave another portion to contribute to your "retirement" fund.

2. Set your (subjective) intertemporal preference

There are no arbitrary ratios. Personally, I ask myself what level of consumption I look for at a certain age and think of a relatively reasonable rate of interest to be earned from investing my net worth at retirement in investment grade debt. Suppose that you want to retire at 62 and your age is 40. You have 22 years to reach your target. Suppose that, in real purchasing power, you believe an annual gross income of $96,000 would be acceptable for your spouse and you, considering you will no longer have to pay rent/mortgage or sustain your offspring. If the $96,000 annual cash flow will be provided by a relatively stable investment in debt, you may assume that the associated interest rate will be 4%.[5] Therefore, by 62, you would need a net worth of $2,400,000. In the majority of cases, people receive an inheritance. Assume the inheritances of both your spouse and yours reach $800,000 or the equivalent of two properties.[6] You have 22 years to save $1,600,000. Earning no interest or compounded returns in the process, it would require approximate annual savings of $73,000. But you expect to earn a compounded return over the next 22 years. We will discuss how to earn it in the following lessons.

Once aforementioned steps 1 and 2 are in place, you should not worry about the volatility of your investment portfolio, to which you add every year, according to step 2, that is, your intertemporal preference.

There are a few implicit, noteworthy points here. Firstly, in step 1, one is correctly acknowledging the role of money. Money is not an investment asset class, as portfolio theory states. Money is an institution that addresses unexpected scenarios, situations that go beyond a limited tree of possibilities. Secondly, going

---

[5] Assuming in the next 22 years we go back to positive real interest rates, away from quantitative easing/zero interest rate policies.

[6] I base this on average Canadian housing prices at the time of this writing.

Steps 1 & 2

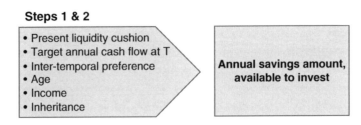

- Present liquidity cushion
- Target annual cash flow at T
- Inter-temporal preference
- Age
- Income
- Inheritance

Annual savings amount, available to invest

Fig. 2.3 Steps 1 and 2

forward, one will not worry about the liquidity characteristics of an asset chosen to invest in. One will not pay a premium for a liquidity that is illusory, in an asset that is not money: Big cap stocks, government debt, etc. (Fig. 2.3).

3. Intertemporal preference is asset allocation

As suggested, to save the target $1,600,000 determined above, the maximum a couple would have to save is $73,000 per year, for 22 years. This is substantial: In 2017, it is more than the average GDP per capita in the United States. The next question is, therefore, **What compounded rate of return is achievable, which from a real (i.e. not financial) point of view, is also reasonable?** This is a key question and constitutes a key departure from portfolio theory and everything you have been taught in a mainstream Finance course.

We are no longer asking ourselves how to obtain alpha (i.e. returns above market). We are separating ourselves from any benchmark. **We are targeting a rate of return. This target rate is separated from any statistical analysis on volatility, any liquidity considerations or policy environment, and is subjective.** In my view, in the twenty-first century and given the speed of technological advances, I believe that a 12% is a reasonable rate.[7]

I would never expect to earn 12% in real terms, from a debt instrument, without ignoring the credit quality of the said instrument. But I believe that a proper mix of equity and debt in my portfolio should be able to produce a 12% return, compounded, and without facing unbearable volatility. A 12% compounded return would require annual contributions of $15,500 approximately per couple, or $7250 per spouse.

The above scenario, in my view, is achievable. The question is how to get to that compounded target return. To obtain it, one has to average the returns of the equity and debt portions of a portfolio. The ratio of equity to debt is,

---

[7] In the nineteenth century, 5% might have been more appropriate, given the lower productivity rates at that time.

again, subjective. It depends on one's intertemporal preferences. **We no longer abuse the theory of probability to get comfortable under the illusion of an optimal portfolio.**[8]

We can think of a market interest rate as:

$$\text{Gross profits } i = \text{Market interest rate} + \text{entrepreneurial profits } i$$

Then,

$$\text{Market interest rate} = \text{Gross profits } i - \text{entrepreneurial profits } i$$

Common retirement planning wisdom advises that the younger you are the more you should allocate to stocks, to equity, rather than bonds. As if under a financial crisis, the correlation between the two asset classes did not spike to 1. The logic behind this advice is that, since you are younger, you can afford to hold volatile securities in exchange for potentially faster net worth growth. You can take risks while you are young. And while this reasoning sounds familiar, remember that it is also a fallacy, based on the misunderstanding of the notion of risk. Risk belongs to limited spaces, to probability theory. When we are young and experiment, we create new, until-then-unknown-to-us worlds. There are no limits. And we are the main actors. When we purchase a public security, we control nothing, except perhaps a stop loss (assuming high-frequency algos don't front-run us).

But the retirement planning wisdom above misinterprets a key aspect of compounded interest, not found in stocks, but in sound debt obligations (no, I am not referring to sovereign debt): For an individual who saves with discipline, the longer the time horizon, the higher the final value. That means that any losses incurred when young will represent enormous final value that is given up (Fig. 2.4).

Another way to see this perspective is this: When you have nothing to lose is when you can bet the most. We all behave differently and with reason when we have nothing to lose. In the current investing context, this means that contrary to popular wisdom, your allocation to volatile investments should increase not the younger but the older you are, **as long as, by that age and in spite of your efforts, you have not saved enough**, which means that there is little you have to lose. An example of this would be a person who is in the low

---

[8] We know that each security we pick is not a random variable: Its returns do not show a frequency; and if there is one, it does not converge to a defined number, nor will it remain stable regardless of what time series we choose.

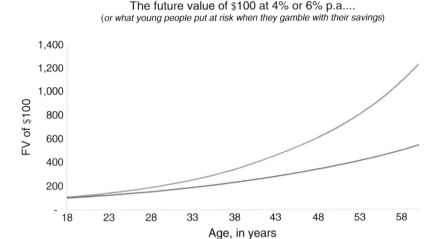

The future value of $100 at 4% or 6% p.a....
(*or what young people put at risk when they gamble with their savings*)

Fig. 2.4 The final value of $100, at 4% (blue) or 6% (orange). (Color figure online)

50s and has barely any savings. **How one assesses that "nothing to lose", again, is a subjective exercise, foreign to all optimization objective analysis.** In my personal case (i.e. at my age and given my financial situation), I believe a 35% allocation to what I deem "dangerous" is appropriate.

Conclusion

Under a correct interpretation of probability theory and of the concept of liquidity, there is no room for optimization. Asset allocation is simply the logical outcome of intertemporal preferences. This begins with the analysis of one's liquidity preference and the target final value of one's savings over a certain time horizon. The younger you are, the more discipline and conservatism (do not misunderstand me: I mean this with regard to investing your savings, but not with regard to taking entrepreneurial risk! Young people *must* be entrepreneurial!) you have to apply to investing, because the final value of $1 given up by careless investing is higher (the younger you are).

Capital

If an interest rate is an intertemporal exchange rate that is the result of a subjective preference, then what is capital? Let's start by stating what capital is not: It is not money. As odd as this sounds, the fact is that John Maynard

Keynes (and his followers) did confuse capital with money. There is compelling proof of this in numerous examples throughout his *General Theory of Employment, Interest and Money*. To illustrate, I propose this paragraph from Chap. 11, on "The Marginal Efficiency of Capital":

> *… The expectation of a fall in the value of money stimulates investment, and hence employment generally, because it raises the schedule of the marginal efficiency of capital, i.e. the investment demand-schedule; and the expectation of a rise in the value of money is depressing, because it lowers the schedule of the marginal efficiency of capital…*

Capital is the market value of capital goods. And capital goods are anything, absolutely anything that serves a human being to achieve an end. If that end is tangible and requires tangible goods to get involved in its production process, these goods are capital goods. If the end is not tangible and requires intangibles to be achieved, those intangibles are also capital goods. It is incorrect to compare capital with the institution of money. To begin, capital is a subjective, teleological notion. What is capital for me may not be for you. For instance, I may decide to play a game of golf to network with someone who I believe will open the doors to a project I am pursuing. For me, the resources I decided to allocate to that four-hour game at the course are capital goods. For you, the game may very well have been mere leisurely consumption. Hence, there is nothing physically intrinsic to the definition of capital. **But it is an unequivocal feature of capital, the fact that it yields or is expected to yield the materialization of an end.** If that end is measurable in the same metrics that the capital is, the ratio between the two will be measurable too, and we will call it return on capital over an arbitrary period of chronological time.

Derivatives, Commodities Are Not Investing Assets

From the previous section, we can conclude that there are asset classes available to investors that cannot be considered capital. This is so either because even if they are used in the production processes of other goods, they are consumed during them, or because they are not part of the process at all. The first case refers to commodities. The second refers to currencies, gold, art or derivatives.[9] In spite of this, nowadays currencies, commodities, gold and

---

[9] I exclude from this classification those derivatives used for hedging purpose. A derivative that is used as a hedge directly associated to an identified asset is a capital good.

derivatives are advertised either directly or indirectly to investors. These asset classes have also been made available to the general public through structured finance products like exchange-traded funds with the excuse of providing diversification or alternative liquid investment options. They may very well be used to gain exposure to specific trading strategies, but I can hardly see myself allocating part of my savings to invest in them. Currencies, art, gold, commodities or derivatives will not yield a by-product, they will not produce income, and therefore, they do not benefit from the wonders of compounding interest. They belong to trading strategies and since my intention is to write about investing (i.e. not trading), I will not discuss them here. But I hope that the following will illustrate my point.

The price of crude oil crashed twice in the past decade: In 2008 and in 2014. In 2008, I made the mistake that I am advising to avoid: I used a structured finance product that, in the end, did not play out as expected. Additionally, the fact that it is not possible to call a bottom or a top in a commodity price brought hurting losses. In 2014, I decided to take the approach just recommended. I would not trade the oil crash but invest in the oil crash. How was this possible? In commodities, a reversal of the trend is reflected in a change of their respective futures "curves", which brings me to explain the concepts of contango and backwardation (Fig. 2.5).

Commodities incur into storage costs, and when we purchase them through futures contracts, the longer the term of the contract, the higher these costs are. Therefore, it is natural to expect the spot price to be higher than futures prices (net of storage costs that is). This is normal, and when it happens, it is

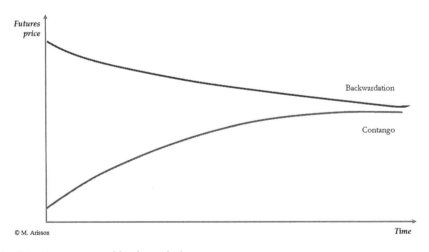

© M. Arisson

Fig. 2.5 Contango and backwardation

said that the respective commodity market is in backwardation. There are times, however, when a sudden change of conditions in a commodity market may force liquidation on the part of the commodity producers. In these cases, precisely because of the costs incurred to store the commodity, producers want to get rid of the commodity inventory at spot prices significantly below that which cleared the market until a day ago. The fall in the spot price can be so serious that the entire futures market curve will shift from backwardation to a positive slope where the spot price is lower than future prices. When this happens, it is said that the respective commodity market entered into contango. A contango market is a bear market (for the commodity).

In the case of crude oil, the crash of 2014 forced those producers with the highest marginal costs to run for the exits, selling whatever inventory they had available, before transportation and storage costs. They had been funding their capital expenditures with debt and needed to protect liquidity and reduce leverage. In so doing, they drove the spot price down, while the long-term price of the barrel remained relatively stable. In other words, crude oil entered in contango. A trader with liquidity could buy spot crude oil today, store it and deliver it at a higher price in the future, making a profit, if he found where to store it, that is. And this is where my investment idea came in. I realized that I could "invest" in the oil crash, rather than trade it, by purchasing what at the time I thought were undervalued public shares of crude oil transportation (i.e. tankers) companies. At the time, I looked for companies that would trade below 15× P/E, would have positive cash flow, distribute a dividend, had low leverage (i.e. Debt/EBITDA < 3.0×) and would have been trading at least a 30% discount from the last 52-week high. This investment idea ended up being one of the best in 2015, regardless of all the volatility in crude oil. I owned equity, to play a specific commodity theme.

Lastly, there are those who argue in favour of derivatives as a way to create synthetic equity or debt.[10] But these structured finance trades lack economic sense. Why not buy the equity and debt directly? The answer is simple: Because direct buying is expensive… it must be funded (with real savings). In other words, the synthetic products are a deficient liquidity structure variation: They promise unrealistic returns (i.e. not based on the title to the underlying cash flows, represented either by the equity or by debt of the respective companies) and can only survive as long as the existing supportive credit conditions that enable them survive. If the underlying securities see their valuations plunge, the run for the exits will be narrow, triggering a downward price spiral until a true, leverage-free price is discovered.

---

[10] An example is the "tranching" of credit indices. Refer footnote No. 71 in Lesson 4.

Investments Versus Trades

In the previous pages, I discussed the impact caused by misleading concepts, which have been commonly accepted and mutated since the beginnings of the age of democracy (i.e. differential analysis, general equilibrium, probability theory, liquidity, high-frequency trading, sovereign risk and beta). I also analysed the relationship between asset allocations and intertemporal preference. The same is guided by interest rates through a social coordination process, which when institutionalized adopts the form of a market (i.e. the savings market), and I provided a definition of what constitutes a capital asset, and what doesn't. It is now time to clarify and understand the difference between an investment and a trade.

An investment is the allocation of one's savings into a capital asset. **An investment delivers a by-product with the mere passage of time**. In an investment, we can single out and therefore distinguish the capital from the yield. An investment does not necessarily belong to a fixed income class. Real assets (e.g. cattle) or equity investments also deliver a "dividend" (preferred or not) and thus fit this definition (more so, if we have control of the dividend policy).

By default, when one allocates one's savings into anything that is not a capital asset, a trade takes place. In a trade, one simply looks for a gain. It must be remembered that both investment and trades are speculative, since both constitute purposeful action, with an end in sight.

From a practical point, the main difference between an investment and a trade is that in a trade we must ex ante and always determine a stop **gain**, that is, an exit point. Always! For both investments and trades, one must establish the thesis, identify driving fundamentals, stop losses and possibly a term horizon. But for trades, one must also fix an exit point (which can be reassessed from time to time) and stand by it. In the case of an investment, however, as long as it yields, it is only valid to exit it if one finds a better investment. **The good investor is the one who can distinguish an investment from a trade and execute accordingly.** Having clarified the difference between an investment and a trade, I want to remind that this book is about investing, not trading.

Bibliography

Markowitz, Harry. (March, 1952). Portfolio Selection. *The Journal of Finance*. Vol. 7, No. 1.

Benes, Jaromir, and Kumhof, Michael (August, 2012). The Chicago Plan Revisited. *IMF Working Paper*. WP 12/202. Washington, DC: International Monetary Fund. Retrieved November 2013 from: http://www.imf.org/external/pubs/ft/wp/2012/wp12202.pdf

Sibileau, Martin. (November, 2012). Why the Chicago Plan is flawed reasoning and would fail. *A View from the Trenches*. Retrieved November 2013 from https://www.zerohedge.com/news/2012-11-11/guest-post-why-chicago-plan-flawed-reasoning-and-would-fail

3

Turing's Decidability

In the previous lesson, we argued that intertemporal preferences determine asset allocation. Once a specific portion of our savings is targeted for equity or debt, we still need to know what equity or what debt securities to purchase. And for this task, we must revert to fundamentals. There is nothing more practical than a good theory: If equity is a property title on entrepreneurship, we must first understand what entrepreneurship is.

Entrepreneurship is innate to all of us.[1] If we don't understand the concept of entrepreneurship, nothing in economics and even less in finance can make sense. To start, an entrepreneur is not a category. Nobody is or isn't an entrepreneur. Rather, entrepreneurship is a skill, which all of us use in varying degrees. To be entrepreneurial means to unleash our innate ability to see, to discover, to materialize an opportunity that may or may not have been available before, and to act upon. Any external constraint on entrepreneurship is a constraint on human nature.

Entrepreneurship is "the" source of information within the market process. However, this information is not explicit, written or available to everyone; it is generally discarded and underestimated. The dismissal of this (non-articulated) knowledge is deeply rooted in our public educational system. One of the objectives of this book, if not the main one, is to make you familiar with it.[2]

---

[1] These comments are based on *Formalizing Austrian Thought: A Suggested Approach*, Revista Procesos de Mercado, Año 2014, Vol. 11, No. 2, Madrid, (b) *Complexity of Algorithms*, Lecture Notes 1999, Peter Gács and László Lovász, Chapter 3, and Huerta de Soto's *The Austrian School: Market Order and Entrepreneurial Creativity*, Edward Elgar Publishing (2008).

[2] For an enjoyable and educating read on the subject, refer Huerta de Soto's *The Austrian School: Market Order and Entrepreneurial Creativity*, Edward Elgar Publishing (2008).

© The Author(s) 2018
M. Arisson, *Investing in the Age of Democracy*,
https://doi.org/10.1007/978-3-319-95903-0_3

Formalization of Entrepreneurship Is an Error

Formalization of entrepreneurship is a constant exercise by finance professionals these days. Notwithstanding, it is a mistake. But let's first define formalization itself. To establish formalization, there are certain necessary conditions against which one could contrast the entrepreneurial phenomenon. Only then it is possible to decide if entrepreneurship can be formalized.

Conditions for formalization have already been established for some time and conform the logical platform underlying computing. Until the 1930s, it was generally believed that as long as a question found a precise description, it would have been possible to solve it with mathematics. But, what was meant by a "precise description"? Two interpretations were put forth. In the first one, one dealt with a "yes/no" question. The decision could be proved or disproved from axioms. But, entrepreneurship, as it is creativity or (in economic terms) a choice of a mean towards an end or an exchange, does not enjoy the benefit of a "yes/no" decision. By definition, there cannot be an ex ante question with regard to entrepreneurship. We cannot accept or deny the existence of an end or a mean that has not yet been created or discovered.

In 1931, the mathematician and logician Kurt Gödel suggested a second interpretation, simultaneously proving that perfectly formulated questions cannot be answered from the axioms of a set theory. It is this second interpretation that interests me: According to Gödel, a "problem" is decidable if it can be solved through a family of questions. If so, we say that an algorithm _**decides**_ it. Is entrepreneurship "decidable"? If it is, it should be formalized.

To answer this question, we must first examine what an algorithm is. An algorithm is a mathematical procedure serving for a computation or construction (the computation of some function), which can be carried out mechanically. This is a formal definition. Before we examine the decidability of entrepreneurship, I suggest to you that any good that is already exchanged and therefore already has economic significance can be conceived as an algorithm. There were a set of instructions that made possible the satisfaction of an economic goal: The good. Now to illustrate, consider an underdeveloped country where there is limited specialization of knowledge and a rancher has to carry out multiple actions down the production chain: A "sirloin beef" is a good that can be thought in the following (relaxed) algorithmic terms (Fig. 3.1):

The instructions above from the first to the last step make it possible to bring a beef to a supermarket shelf. If an economic good is, formally speaking, an algorithm, **entrepreneurship is a process in which humans seek to discover and build algorithms that solve or decide "problems"** (even though

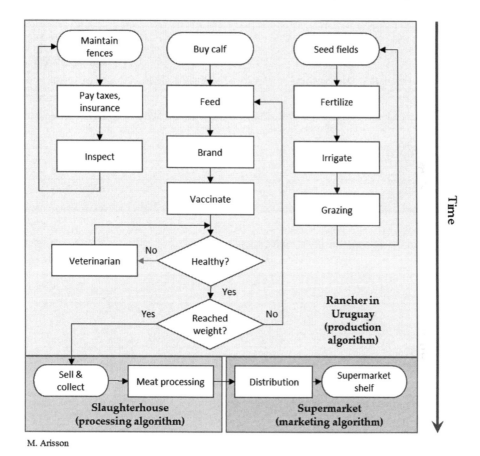

M. Arisson

Fig. 3.1 The good "sirloin beef" conceived as an algorithm

a "problem" may also have to be discovered or created). But this second inter-pretation poses an ontological challenge, and if we are to use mathematics to analyse human action, we must answer the following questions:

(a) What is the mathematical notion of an algorithm?
(b) How do we define "algorithmic solvability"?

In separate ways, these questions were answered during the 1930s by two mathematicians and logicians: Alonzo Church (1903–1995) and Alan Turing (1912–1954). Church developed the notion of recursive functions, while Turing that which is known today as a "Turing machine". The notions are equivalent and they both succeed at mathematically defining algorithms, but here I will discuss recursive functions.

In computation theory, a finite set of symbols is called an alphabet. A finite sequence formed from elements of such alphabet is called a word. And an arbitrary set of words is called a language. Formally, we say that **a language L is recursive if its characteristic function is recursive**[3]:

$$FL(x) = \{1, \text{if } x \in L \text{ or } 0, \text{otherwise}$$

In this case, we can also say that L is decidable (if a language L is recursive, its complement is also recursive). **But, what does all this have to do with investing?** Investing can only be executed using accounting. And accounting, under the above definitions, is a recursive language. Think of a function that we shall call "profit function", with words like "price", "unit cost", "quantity", "overhead costs" and "taxes" such that:

$$\text{Profit}(X) = \left[\text{price}(x) - \text{unit cost}(x) \right] \\ * \text{quantity}(x) - \text{overhead}(x) - \text{taxes}(x)$$

Accounting is a recursive and decidable language, for we can use the composite function:

$$G\left[\text{profit}(x) \right] = \{1, \text{if } x \in L \text{ or } 0, \text{otherwise}$$

$G(x)$ returns a 1, if profit (x) is a positive number, or zero, if profit (x) returns is not positive (i.e., a loss). Note that when we state that $G(x) = 1$ if $x \in L$, we are essentially saying that $G(x)$ returns a profit if x belongs to an _already existing_ going concern. **$G(x)$ represents a process related to deciding "problem" (x).** But accounting is simply a language. **What is relevant and should not be lost to the investor is that profit (x) does not come to exist ex nihilo.** Profit (x) is created by entrepreneurial activity, and it raises an ontological question: **Is this entrepreneurial activity in itself also recursive or decidable?** It is not: When it comes to deciding ends, it is not possible to isolate a set of symbols within a language to characterize it. The sentence "$x \in L$" is not decidable. We cannot say that an object "x" that may or may not have been existing at the time we pose this question belongs or not to a production process. For instance, until the 1960s, we could have not affirmed that:

---

[3] The symbol "∈" means "belongs to". Thus, "_if_ $x \in L$" means "if x belongs to L".

$$Silicon \in \text{Intel's production function}$$

Yet silicon existed, but it was not an input for a production function corresponding to a firm called Intel. Silicon is a material, but it lacked its economic relevance as a resource for that production function. It was entrepreneurship, which gave it economic meaning. The means used to obtain certain ends do not return a clear duality {0, 1}, because means are subjective and ends can also be means, which until a moment ago did not exist. **Hence, entrepreneurship is not decidable**.

Decidability and Finance

Entrepreneurship is not a decidable phenomenon, and because of this, it cannot be formalized. This conclusion should have relevant implications for the theory of Finance. The first immediate implication, in my view, is that if entrepreneurship cannot be formalized, it could also not be valued.

However, there is a more relevant implication. Entrepreneurship may not be decidable, but the result of it, the created object, is. Once the entrepreneur creates an ongoing concern, he **makes a problem decidable**, via a composite function, which we can call G **[profit (x)]** and which holds **ex-post** (i.e. after the entrepreneurial act).

We are familiarized with the adjective "mature", given to a business model. When one speaks of a "mature" business, what one refers to is a specific algorithm that not only includes the production process corresponding to that business, but also that of marketing and financial strategies. These processes, in our terms, are decidable. One can therefore think of different degrees of decidability corresponding to different businesses. **A good hint on the undecidability of a business model is the status of the accounting rules applied to it. When a business is very undecidable, the different accounting colleges or boards have to develop accounting standards and definitions on how to measure and account for its revenue.** The production processes of cheese or wine are mature. They are decidable. But their different marketing strategies are less decidable. It is perhaps this difference in decidability within different competitors what makes some entrepreneurs win market share at the expense of others.

At the other extreme, one can think of Google Inc. as the showcase of undecidability in business. Google's mission is:

> ...to organize the world's information and make it universally accessible and useful...

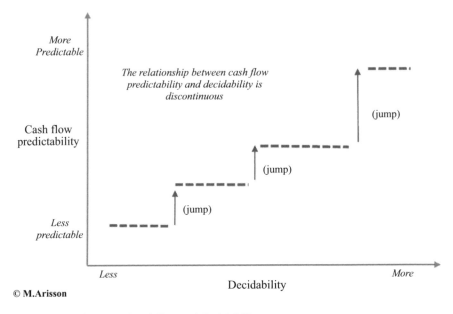

Fig. 3.2 Cash flow predictability and decidability

How do we know what can be considered information? What does it mean to make it universally accessible, let alone useful?

No company will ever be completely decidable or undecidable, but it will exhibit different degrees of decidability. **The higher the degree of decidability, the easier it will be to understand and predict its cash flow generation, if any**. However, we must note here that although that prediction may be possible, one cannot assign a probability to it, as discussed earlier.[4] Each business is a unique historical event. It is not a collective; its cash flow does not exhibit a relative frequency, let alone a convergence to a specific figure. And if it did, it would not pass the test of randomness.[5] **Therefore, we can predict but not assign a probability** (Fig. 3.2).

The connection between decidability and finance is fundamental: The higher the degree of decidability in a business, the easier it will be to understand and predict its performance (i.e. margins, attainable leverage, capital structure, etc.). An entrepreneur is anyone who creates decidable problems or discovers previously undecidable problems and transforms them into decidable ones.

---

[4] To be able to recur to probability theory, one must refer to a properly defined collective. A collective must fulfil two conditions: (a) the relative frequencies of particular attributes within a collective must converge to fixed limits, and (b) the fixed limits must not be affected by any place selection.

[5] Measured in different periods, said convergence would change.

Decidability and Capital Structure

At this point, we can summarize some of our main propositions.

Proposition	Implications
1 Human action is discreet, not continuous	Discard infinitesimal analysis
2 Social coordination is dynamic	Discard general equilibrium models
3 Companies are unique, unrepeatable events	Discard probability theory
4 Liquidity is not an asset's attribute	Do not pay a liquidity premium
5 Sovereign defaults exist; inflation is default	There is no risk-free return
6 Sovereign defaults are independent from corporate defaults	Asset returns should not be added to sovereign returns
7 Asset returns are not random (i.e. Brownian) processes	Optimization and efficiency are tautological
8 Interest rates are rates of intertemporal exchange	Asset allocation is subjective intertemporal preference
9 Entrepreneurship is not decidable	Equity valuation is tautological
10 Decidability determines cash flow predictability	Decidability determines capital structure

Point #10 above is the direct logical outcome of our previous discussion on Turing's decidability. In the 1950s, (mainstream) economists Franco Modigliani and Merton Miller developed a theorem[6] which states that under certain conditions the value of the firm is independent of how it is financed. Like other theorems in Finance, this one was based on an immaculate firm, conceived without sin. Control and politics never played any consideration. In other words, they are completely devoid of any, absolutely any, economic sense. They can never explain why firms within the same industry, jurisdiction and so on exhibit different capital structures. If they do, the justification is based on taxes that are distorting, or because bankruptcy, reputation or information costs exist. To describe this state of affairs, some economists say that markets are inefficient! This is no different from the approach ancient Greek philosophers took to examine reality: They first came up with ideals, and reality was studied only in so far as facts approached these ideals. If the facts were far from ideal, they were called "impure". Today, they are called "inefficient" (suggesting that central planning and intervention can improve the status quo). There cannot be neutrality or indifference in the capital structure of a company. For the company owners, issuing shares to raise capital means that their control on the company is diluted, while at the same time, no conditions are imposed to them by inves-

---

[6] Modigliani, F.; Miller, M. (1958). *The Cost of Capital, Corporation Finance and the Theory of Investment*, American Economic Review.

tors, with regard to liquidity, leverage, security and more. On the other hand, raising debt means that the control is not compromised (as long as the debt covenants, if any, are met), but a commitment must be held, to meet minimum liquidity requirements. For investors, buying equity gives unlimited gains and no floor on losses, until the entire investment is wiped out. Buying debt means stability of income, within an uncertainty that sometimes can (if they can amend the credit agreement) or cannot be managed—but with capped gains.

It is a fallacy to think that investing and financing decisions are independent. Ask yourself whether Elon Musk, Henry Ford or Steve Jobs would have built their dream companies, had they had to compromise control over them for the sake of obtaining funding. Ask yourself if you would value your house differently if it is fully yours or the bank's you mortgaged it to. The utility provided for an observer is the same: it will not change a bit either in the inside or outside. For the person living in it, whether he owns it or not, it makes a complete difference.

Understanding the concept of decidability guides us, investors, to decide in which part of the capital structure it makes sense to invest once we have identified a company. The less decidable its business model is, the less sense it makes to lend to a company and to force it to commit to a series of payments of principal and interest. On the other hand, if we like said company, it makes a lot more sense to invest in its equity (Fig. 3.3).

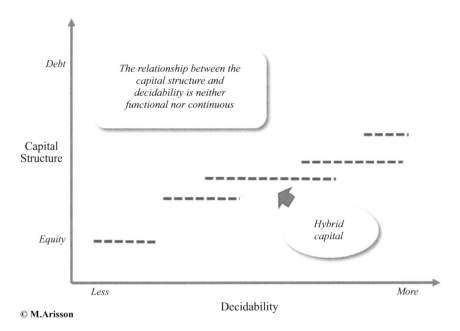

© M.Arisson

Fig. 3.3 Capital structure and decidability

Portfolio Construction

Making a capital structure decision should not be the first decision within the investing process. As we wrote about in the previous lesson, the investment process starts with an allocation decision, based on subjective intertemporal preference. This consists in forecasting our liquidity needs and allocating money to satisfy them in the first place. This will signal how much is left available to invest. Our intertemporal preferences will determine how much to allocate to equity, in one extreme, and debt, in the other (hybrid capital, in any form, goes in between) because of the relationship between targeted returns and those expected from different asset classes.[7] Once we identify those business models or investment themes that interest us, we can map them according to their decidability. This is a purely subjective exercise. Finally, if we are investing in public markets (*more on this in Lessons 5 and 6*), we assign specific companies to each one of the themes to make the investment allocation decision.

Personally, for the last stage, I have defined my own criteria for name selection: A mix of technicals and fundamentals. If more than one name meets them, I split my target portfolio allocation among them. Prudence tells me that I should have a single name/business model/investment theme allocation limit (Fig. 3.4).

Mezzanine Investing: Avoid It

In the previous graphs, we saw that as decidability in an enterprise increases, it makes sense to finance it less with equity and more with debt. But there is an area between the two extremes (in decidability), which is difficult to evaluate. Because this place is in the middle and the Italian word for "middle" is "mezzo", that area is called "mezzanine". Mezzanine financing or the idea of financing a company with neither pure debt nor pure equity became popular in the twentieth century when capital structure arbitraging began in earnest.

---

[7] In this case, given the collective "asset classes", it is legitimate to use probability theory. To begin with, one can expect with confidence that the return of the asset class "equity" shall be higher than that of the asset class "debt". Otherwise, there would be no entrepreneurship.

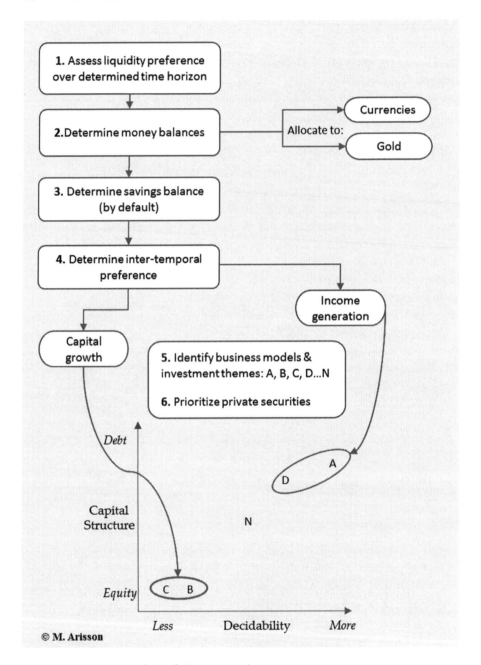

Fig. 3.4   The (subjective) portfolio construction process

Mezzanine financing can also be carried out with leverage via synthetic structures.[8] But if it is not possible to use probability to evaluate outcomes from investing in equity, it must be true that it is even more difficult to judge the wisdom of investing in a mezzanine instrument, let alone a leveraged or synthetic one. Yet, even pension funds are long mezzanine tranches in synthetic credit structures. This is not investing but simply trading.[9]

----

[8]

Structured capital structure: The case of a tranched credit index (Example: CDX.NA.HY Index in 2017)

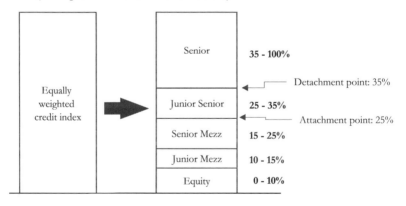

[9] I think investing in (private, not public) mezzanine only makes sense if you are a lawyer, looking for work.

Appendix I: Monetary Policy and Capital Structure

Interestingly, the so-called quantitative easing (QE) policies of the twenty-first century shed light on the impact of monetary policy on capital structure decisions. QE, in the United States, consists in monetizing US federal government deficits:

Fig. 3.5 Balance sheets of the Fed and US government under QE

In Fig. 3.5, the amount of US dollars in circulation increases when US sovereign debt is purchased by the Fed. The US dollars created are subsequently deposited in the banking system and the wonders of fractional reserve expand them multiple times. In so doing, the "loan" interest rate drops. But since 2009, given the magnitude of QE and the impact of the Basel III regulatory framework, the loan interest rate dropped so significantly that the profitability of the banking system plunged. Forced by law to increase capital and liquidity, and with lower interest rate margins, corporate banks embarked on a path of steady diminishing returns, protected by a blanket of lower expected loan losses. This situation led banks to look beyond common places, to lend to high-yield companies. In so doing, they reversed the natural relationship between decidability and capital structure, discussed in this lesson. Banks, partly funded themselves with demand deposits and partly with debt, could only remain profitable if they earned additional investment banking fees. Therefore, roles reversed and banks became de facto the new providers of venture capital for those sectors that could afford capital markets services (i.e. origination, advisory, hedging). They are usually undecidable ventures and the flavour of the day at that time[10] happened to be the US and Canadian oil and gas shale, exploration and production companies. Within the exploration and production (E&P) sub-space, the reversal in the decidability/capital structure suffered the most. The vehicle was secured lending in the form of borrowing base credit lines (Figs. 3.6, 3.7):

Indeed, the crash in the price of oil and gas was caused by factors beyond monetary policy. But, had the profitability of the banking sector not been decimated by regulations, banks would have not been pushed to the borrowing base lending sector in the volumes and at the prices they did. The contagion that took place during 2015 would have thus been much more limited.

---

[10] The oil crisis of the twenty-first century had its origins in the productivity gains created by shale fracking, in the United States and Canada. This obviously led to an oversupply.

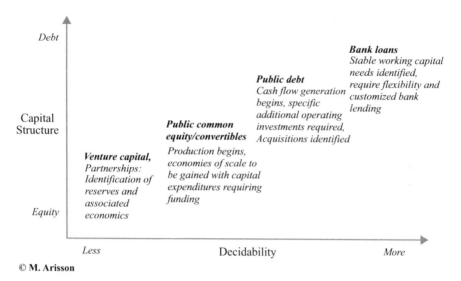

Fig. 3.6 Oil exploration and production *without* quantitative easing, under normal conditions

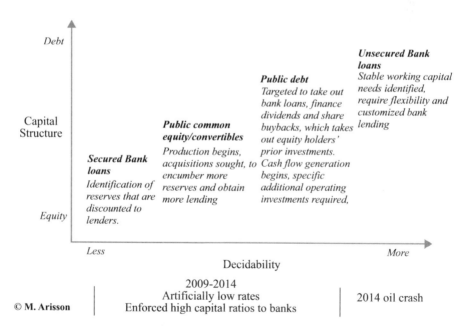

Fig. 3.7 Oil exploration and production *with* quantitative easing and Basel III: The recipe for a lending crisis caused by policy makers

Appendix II: Decidability and Economies of Scale

In any regular course of microeconomics, economies of scale may be formalized using the following function:

$$Y = A L^\alpha K^\beta$$

Where:

Y = total production (the real value of all goods produced)
L = labour input (the total number of person-hours worked)
K = capital input (the real value of all machinery, equip.)
A = total factor productivity
α and β are the output elasticities of capital and labour, respectively. These
    values are constants determined by available technology.

If

$$\alpha + \beta = 1,$$

The production function has constant returns to scale, meaning that doubling the usage of capital K and labour L will also double output Y.
For example, when capital and labour double:

$$A \left(2 \times L\right)^\alpha \left(2 \times K\right)^\beta =$$
$$A\, 2^\alpha \times L^\alpha \times 2^\beta \times K^\beta =$$
$$A\, 2^{(\alpha+\beta)} \times L^\alpha\, K^\beta$$

With $a + \beta = 1$ and reorganizing $2\,A\,L^\alpha\,K^\beta = 2\,Y$, which shows that Y (i.e. production) doubles too.
It is therefore easy to see that if:

$$\alpha + \beta < 1, \text{ returns to scale are decreasing,}$$

And if:

$$\alpha + \beta > 1, \text{ returns to scale are increasing.}$$

The above equation is known as the Cobb-Douglas production function, after Paul Douglas and Charles Cobb.[11] It assumes that there is already a decidable production process that has been identified, which by way of inputting fixed factors of production in a given proportion delivers the produce with a given return. This is by all means a mechanistic view, devoid of any economic sense. But this perspective has been taught and used for so long that we have come to believe in it unquestionably. It doesn't have any economic sense because, to begin with, it is static. It does not explain how a product came to be, nor how will it remain competitive in the market. In other words, it completely misses the role of entrepreneurship and it assumes no flexibility in terms of resource reallocation. **The fact that we cannot formalize such flexibility is not an excuse to ignore it.**

With the development of information technology and the internet, a concept similar to "economies of scale" appeared, although this time it did have economic sense. I am referring to the concept of a "platform". In a way, an online platform is a social institution. Its value derives from the spontaneous social cooperation that it brings to life and is therefore, **by its very nature, a concrete form of undecidability. The fact that online platforms are valued by investors is proof that we humans acknowledge the concept of decidability. It is the cooperation that a platform enables what makes it a scalable resource, in a true economic, not mechanistic sense. As an investor, this is the real economies of scale that I look for in my investments allocated to equity.**

Bibliography

Sibileau, Martin. (2014). *Formalizing Austrian Thought: A suggested approach*. Madrid: Revista Procesos de Mercado, Año 2014, Vol. 11, No. 2.

Gács, Peter (Boston University) and Lovász, László (Yale University). (Spring 1999). *Complexity of Algorithms*. Lecture Notes. Retrieved March 2013 from http://web.cs.elte.hu/~lovasz/complexity.pdf

Modigliani, F. and Miller, M. (June 1958). The Cost of Capital, Corporation Finance and the Theory of Investment. *American Economic Review*. Vol. 48, No. 3, pp. 261–297.

---

[11] Cobb, Charles W. (Amherst College) and Douglas, Paul H. (Univ. Of Chicago), *A Theory of Production*, The American Economic Review, Vol. 18, No. 1, Supplement, Papers and Proceedings of the Fortieth Annual Meeting of the American Economic Association (Mar., 1928), pp. 139–165. Found at: http://www.jstor.org/stable/1811556?seq=1#page_scan_tab_contents

Cobb, Charles W. (Amherst College) and Douglas, Paul H. (Univ. Of Chicago). (March, 1928). A Theory of Production. *The American Economic Review.* Vol. 18, No. 1, Supplement, Papers and Proceedings of the Fortieth Annual Meeting of the American Economic Association, pp. 139. Retrieved January 2015 from http://www.jstor.org/stable/1811556?seq=1#page_scan_tab_contents

Huerta de Soto, Jesús. (2008). *Market Order and Entrepreneurial Creativity.* Cheltenham, UK: Edward Elgar Publishing.

4

Equity

Equity is the (legal) title on an entrepreneurial undertaking As an outside investor who holds a fraction of the equity of an identified company, I do not have the entrepreneurial knowledge necessary to estimate the outcome of the initiatives undertaken by the company. I am not the entrepreneur. I can still have an opinion, but by definition, I shall know less than the founder, who is the entrepreneur. Therefore, my valuation on the same will always be based on already known and past information. This is so because, by definition, entrepreneurial activity is not decidable. When equity analysts unfold their valuation scenarios with sensitivities to revenues or costs or any other value driver, they are simply running a circular exercise, where they demonstrate the consequences of what they have already assumed.

If I state:

$$y = x + 2$$

I am already stating that the pair (4; 2) or the pair (1,000,002; 1,000,000) complies with my statement. I am certainly not providing a proof in any case. Likewise, if I state that for a certain company revenue is to grow by 15% annually, with an EBITDA margin that I estimate will be 20%, in an equity market that I think will pay a 10× EBITDA multiple, I am not proving anything new about the value of that company. I am simply running a circularity, for in $t + 1$, the set ($10.0MM, $11.5MM, $2,3MM, $23MM, t0) is as valid a result as ($5MM, $5.75MM, $1.15MM, $11,5MM) for any vector (sales t, sales $t + 1$, EBITDA/sales $t + 1$, Equity value $t + 1$).

© The Author(s) 2018
M. Arisson, *Investing in the Age of Democracy*,
https://doi.org/10.1007/978-3-319-95903-0_4

Analysts address this circularity applying probability weights. They will not consider a simple scenario, but say three (i.e. worst, base and best). They next assign a probability to each of them, where the sum of all three probabilities adds up to 1. This is a mistake. It is only possible to speak about probabilities in reference to a properly defined collective. And a collective must fulfil two conditions: (a) the relative frequencies of particular attributes within a collective must tend to fixed limits, and (b) the fixed limits must not be affected by any place selection. When making a valuation, it is not possible to make the case that a particular company in a specific segment, with unique management and products, is indeed a collective. Even more obvious should be that as a unique historical case, the attributes driving the value of that company do not exhibit relative frequencies and that if they did, they would be affected by a change in management or markets in which the company operates.

The circularity just exposed is absent when we value the debt part of a firm's capital structure because the redemption value of debt is capped at 100% of the principal owed by the firm. When one values debt, one is interested in assessing the likelihood that a firm will or will not default. And if it does, one has to value what the loss will be, given the default. Indeed, it is not possible to argue that different companies, with different products, management and markets conform to a collectible. But they imperfectly do so when it comes to certain attributes: For example, leverage (i.e. debt/earnings) and interest coverage. It is valid to make a judgement on the relative likelihood of default by companies within a sector, with similar attributes. But such a judgement is purely speculation on our part, and as important, no values can be assigned to probabilities.

However, today, there are software applications based on so-called structural models[1] that claim to be capable of assigning a value to these likelihoods, which they mistake for probabilities. These applications assume that the volatility of equity returns, that is, past information, is a collective attribute. And they seek to measure their frequency distribution to evaluate how probable it is for a firm to see the value of its assets fall to that critical point where they equal that of its liabilities: If assets = liabilities, then equity = 0, and the firm is in default.

An additional assumption these applications make is that the value of liabilities remains static. But when firms run into liquidity problems, negotiations take place between them and their lenders. Covenants are amended,

---

[1] For instance, see M. R. Grasselli and T. R. Hurd, *Credit Risk Modeling*, McMaster University, Hamilton, January, 2010: "*Under structural models, a default event is deemed to occur for a firm when its assets reach a sufficiently low level compared to its liabilities. These models require strong assumptions on the dynamics of the firm's asset, its debt and how its capital is structured.*"

events of default are waived, debt is refinanced or alternative investors are proposed. It is therefore inexcusable to apply probability theory to such a process, as the same lenders that seek to assess the probability of a default in their portfolio have the capacity to alter outcomes, and the attributes used for the measurements are simply unrepeatable, unique historical events (i.e. volatility, which in public markets, is mostly driven by macro events proper of fiat currency systems). For the involved lenders, there is hardly anything of a stochastic nature during a downward credit migration process.

How is it possible that we have had (and still have) equity and debt analysts for the past century? It is perfectly possible and history is proof that we can continue to have them. Men abhor uncertainty. Our nature is not perfect and is filled with dangers that we cannot foresee. For this reason, since times immemorial and in all the early civilizations, there has been a group of men and women who made a living foretelling the future. Oracles in Mediterranean islands or Mayan priests in forbidden towns (i.e. Tulum) have equally kept alive the illusion that it is possible to methodically evaluate future outcomes.

When the outcomes were of a mechanical—that is, not human—nature, we devised models to simplify concepts. And even when such models misrepresent reality, it is generally accepted that their use is better than nothing, in the face of complete ignorance. Such is the case of the Ptolemaic astronomical model, in which the Earth was assumed to be the centre of the universe and the planets around it had circular, not elliptical, orbits. One example in modern times is the Black-Scholes model, where for the sake of simplicity one assumes that we live in a world where a riskless asset exists, that it is priced not in the interest rate market but in the money market (a confusion inherited and legitimized by the work of Keynes), that the price of assets are random variables and vary in infinitesimal terms, that stocks do not pay dividends, that money can be borrowed in any infinitesimal amount and without transaction costs, and that randomness exists and exhibits the attributes of a normally distributive function (Fig. 4.1).

Just like in the past, when the Ptolemaic paradigm was challenged, today any challenge to the scientific approach in finance will be met with vigorous opposition.

At this point, one has to ask how it is possible to value either the equity portion or the debt portion of a firm's capital structure. The simple answer is that it is not possible to come to a conclusion about their value in absolute terms. But this should not disappoint, because one should invest in either (or both) equity and debt, recognizing the limitations discussed above. These limitations are best dealt with when the investments are done privately rather than in the public markets.

Fig. 4.1 The Ptolemaic idea of the universe. (Source: The Project Gutenberg EBook of Astronomy of To-day, by Cecil G. Dolmage, image made available by The Internet Archive/American Libraries)

When I invest in private equity, I am either the founder of the company issuing the equity or can have control of the company. At worst, I have fluid communication with the management of the company. If I am not solving the problems faced by the company, at least I am aware of them in real time or can have influence on those who are in charge of solving them. This degree of control is not available to the investor in public equity. And yet, public equity markets have prospered, particularly since the creation of the Federal Reserve (at the end of 1913), which is no coincidence.

The private equity investor is farther ahead of the public equity investor when it comes to overcoming the uncertainties proper of entrepreneurship. Similarly, a direct lender or an investor in private placements is undoubtedly in a better position than the investor in public debt (i.e. secondary loan and bond markets). Direct lenders (i.e. originators) negotiate the credit agreement and interact with management of the issuer to form a first-hand impression on the borrower's repayment capacity. In the credit agreement, they set covenants and the structure and subordination of the loan. This is not permissible to someone buying (public) debt in the secondary market. And yet, just like the market for public equity has grown exponentially, that of public debt continues to grow unabated.

The impressive growth of public markets is a feature of the twentieth century. To the current policy maker of a Ministry of Finance, educated in the mainstream tradition, developed public markets are synonym of liquidity, economic growth and stability.[2] He believes that a centrally planned and regulated capital market will "boost" liquidity, provide a cushion against so-called exogenous shocks and be an engine for economic growth. In fact, exactly the opposite is true. Subsidized and regulated public capital markets distort the concept of and redistribute liquidity, and they amplify shocks. There is no connection between economic growth and public markets. Most would argue that the United States became a superpower in the twentieth century as their public debt and equity markets were growing. But I suggest that the United States was already a much healthier and stronger super power in 1914, with smaller public capital markets, than it was in 2014. In other words, the United States became the world's financial centre *in spite of* public capital markets.

What is the reason for the growth of public capital markets since the twentieth century? In the case of equity, for its market to become public two fundamental features are required: The existence of limited liability and the illusion that insider information is suppressed by proper regulation.

Limited Liability

The innovation of limited liability is believed to have developed with the first European chartered companies, in the seventeenth century. Most notably, the East India Company is put forth as the first one to have benefited from limited liability. But thanks to the tenacity of Prof. Ulrike Malmendier, we know that limited liability had already been instituted at the time of Roman Republic,[3] as an advantage for a specific type of companies known under the name of "*publicani*".[4]

The birth of limited liability is linked to public companies. Indeed, at the beginning of the seventeenth century in Holland, Hugo Grotius (1583–1645) and later Johannes Voet (1647–1713) realized that unlimited liability was a deterrent for the big trading companies to raise funds publicly (i.e. East India Company, United Amsterdam Company). Until that time, the western world continued to borrow from Roman law, which did not acknowledge limited liability.

---

[2] For an illustration of this point, refer the subject and content of the conferences recently held by the Bank of International Settlements. In particular, *Developing corporate bond markets in Asia, BIS Papers No 26, February 2006:* https://www.bis.org/publ/bppdf/bispap26.pdf

[3] From the fifth century BC to the time of the Imperium.

[4] *Ulrike Malmendier, Societas Publicanorum, Staatliche Wirtschaftsactivitätenin den Händen privater Unternehmer, 2002, Böhlau Verlag.*

Under Roman law, creditors had remedy through two actions. One of them was the *actio exercitoria*.[5] In the Justinian's Digest (D. 14.1.17 pr-2, Africanus 8 quaestionum), we learn about the liability of a certain Lucius Titius, who had appointed a Stichus as captain of a ship. In order to prove Titius' liability in the face of Stichus' default, the creditor needed to prove that the purpose of the loan to Stichus, captain, was within the terms of Stichus' contract (*praepositio*). In other words, it was the borrowing cause what was inquired to determine the extent of liability. Grotius therefore realized that the actio exercitoria was an obstacle to the development of maritime trading.[6] It was in this context and at that time, that Holland innovated, limiting the value of liability to the value of the ship and its cargo.[7] The principal or exercitor in a maritime enterprise would now be relieved of all debts arising from a captain's contract or actions if he was willing to cede his whole share and all rights in the ship, including equipment, to the creditor. Voet also shared this view, since he:

> *Thought it excessively harsh that one person should be liable for the contract or actions of another beyond what he had entrusted to his responsibility or care*[8]

From this we can conclude that the renaissance of limited liability took place as a privilege extended by monarchs, rather than as a natural market development, which suggests that investors, as outsiders in a maritime enterprise, were not ready to part with their monies unless those responsible guaranteed their projects with their own possessions.[9] They demanded symmetry in sharing the uncertainties of the enterprise. And in the seventeenth century, maritime trading was an undecidable business.

Finally, Voet reached another important conclusion (outside delictual considerations):

> *With the advent of a strict financial limit, it is interesting to note that the extensive duty of inquiry placed by Roman law on those dealing with a ship's captain can be abandoned. Voet notes that now the only requirements are that one should, knowing*

---

[5] David Johnston, *Limiting Liability: Roman Law and the Civil Law Tradition*, 70 Chi.-Kent. L. Re. 1515 (1995). Available at: http://scholarship.kentlaw.iit.edu/cklawreview/vol70/iss4/6

[6] H. Grotius, *De Iure belli ac pacis* 2.11.13.

[7] Ibid: *"...Ad aestimationem navis et eorum quae in navi sunt..."*

[8] Voet, Commentarius 14.1.5: *dum durum nimis creditum, ex alieno ailum contractu factove teneri ultra id, quod ejus fidei curaeque permisit.*

[9] Prof. Bastos has kindly referred me to the work of Piet-Hein van Eeghen on this topic.

someone to be a ship's captain, lend money to him as such in good faith for the pur-
poses of navigation, and not laboring, under supina ignorantia. Voet states that the
reason this requirement suffices is: (i) because the liability of the exercitor is no longer
unlimited, but limited by the value of the ship and its equipment; (ii) because few
people know what manner, quantity, size, and nature of equipment is necessary for
any given ship, and few will lend to a ship's captain if they have to know it; and (iii)
because the greater fault rests with the exercitor for appointing a cheat as a
captain.[10]

In other words, without the protections of limited liability, investors would not be willing to irresponsibly invest their savings. And because it feels so good to be relieved of such responsibility, in the beginning, monarchs correctly realized that granting such relief had value. Hence, they charged for it: It was a privilege granted to only a few. It was indeed a formidable barrier to entry, which to this day has crowded out others also looking for capital.[11]

I will finish this section by quoting Adam Smith,[12] to give a sense of proportion on the historical relevance of this point (highlighting is mine):

V.1.104
Joint stock companies, established by royal charter or by act of parliament, differ in several respects, not only from regulated companies, but from private copartneries.

First, in a private copartnery, no partner, without the consent of the company, can transfer his share to another person, or introduce a new member into the company. Each member, however, may, upon proper warning, withdraw from the copartnery, and demand payment from them of his share of the common stock. In a joint stock company, on the contrary, no member can demand payment of his share from the company; but each member can, without their consent, transfer his share to another person, and thereby introduce a new member. The value of a share in a joint stock is always the price which it will bring in the market; and this may be either greater or less, in any proportion, than the sum which its owner stands credited for in the stock of the company.

Secondly, in a private copartnery, each partner is bound for the debts contracted by the company to the whole extent of his fortune. In a joint stock company, on the contrary, each partner is bound only to the extent of his share.

---

[10] Ibid., D. Johnston (1995) and Voet, Commentarius, 14.1.6.

[11] In the twenty-first century, compliance with Basel III and Dodd Frank legislation also constitute a barrier to entry and will most likely not be challenged in court by those favoured by it (i.e. those established institutions that can afford to cover the related costs and in the future, pass it on to customers).

[12] *"An Inquiry into the Nature and Causes of the Wealth of Nations"* Book V, Chapter I, 1776.

The trade of a joint stock company is always managed by a court of directors. This court, indeed, is frequently subject, in many respects, to the control of a general court of proprietors. **But the greater part of those proprietors seldom pretend to understand anything of the business of the company, and when the spirit of faction happens not to prevail among them, give themselves no trouble about it, but receive contentedly such half-yearly or yearly dividend as the directors think proper to make to them. This total exemption from trouble and from risk, beyond a limited sum, encourages many people to become adventurers in joint stock companies, who would, upon no account, hazard their fortunes in any private copartnery. Such companies, therefore, commonly draw to themselves much greater stocks than any private copartnery can boast of.** *The trading stock of the South Sea Company, at one time, amounted to upwards of thirty-three millions eight hundred thousand pounds. The divided capital of the Bank of England amounts, at present, to ten millions seven hundred and eighty thousand pounds.* **The directors of such companies, however, being the managers rather of other people's money than of their own, it cannot well be expected that they should watch over it with the same anxious vigilance with which the partners in a private copartnery frequently watch over their own.** *Like the stewards of a rich man, they are apt to consider attention to small matters as not for their master's honour, and very easily give themselves a dispensation from having it. Negligence and profusion, therefore, must always prevail, more or less, in the management of the affairs of such a company.* **It is upon this account that joint stock companies for foreign trade have seldom been able to maintain the competition against private adventurers. They have, accordingly, very seldom succeeded without an exclusive privilege, and frequently have not succeeded with one. Without an exclusive privilege they have commonly mismanaged the trade. With an exclusive privilege they have both mismanaged and confined it.**

Insider Information

Insider information was the key theme in the movie *Wall Street* (1987),[13] where the eternal character Gordon Gekko, personified by Michael Douglas, succinctly told Bud Fox, "*If you're not inside, you are outside*". Gordon was right and many fail to realize that insider knowledge is only natural. It's another manifestation of entrepreneurial knowledge. It is neither good nor bad but only natural that those who are involved in the daily operations of a

---

[13] https://youtu.be/WR5P-mfJU_E

company will count with more information than those who are not. The opposite would be the odd thing. And because ambition is in our nature, it is also reasonable to expect that those with more information than the rest will use it to their own benefit.

Behind the prohibition of insider trading is the idea that it is legitimate to expect fairness when trading public securities. The reason for this expectation escapes me: Why would one provide capital to a company whose management one does not know (and even less influence), in which one has no voting rights unless one holds a significant participation? Of course, the answer is that one would do that because one hopes someone else will buy one out later at a higher price and, if possible, will receive a nice dividend while waiting. But if so, why would one expect fairness? Instead, one should recognize that there is the possibility of suffering a loss due to insider trading. It is a likelihood that should be reflected in the relative value of private versus public securities. Hence, public securities, ceteris paribus, should trade at a discount to private ones to compensate for the lack of control and lack of transparency they offer. Yet, today, the opposite is true: Private trades at a discount to public. And this is a problem because it is certainly not fair to risk one's capital to insiders without compensation. However, investors have a false sense of confidence and believe that insider trading is a so-called tail risk[14] because governments make it illegal. Rather than allowing the price differential between public and private securities to signal investors the dangers at stake, governments simply establish a cap on the cost of breaking the law. Whenever the benefits of breaking the law surpass the associated capped costs (weighted by the perceived likelihood of getting caught), insiders will take a chance. The likelihood of this happening increases considerably when the value of the capital of a company is subject to high volatility because the benefits of inside trading increase while the associated costs (fines, penalties) remain unchanged.

When governments ban insider trading, an important signal is suppressed. If the spread between public and private securities was not suppressed, those issuing securities publicly would be encouraged to narrow the gap, following their self-interest. This effort at coordinating demand and supply of capital is currently absent, and it triggers a series of unforeseen consequences that are beyond the scope of this book.

This brings at least two legitimate questions: Why is insider trading suppressed? And why do public securities trade at a premium (i.e. not at par) against private securities?

---

[14] In probability theory, tail risk refers to the probability of an event occurring that is, say, higher than three standard deviations from its mean. Obviously, as human action is not stochastic, it makes no sense to talk about a tail risk associated to a certain behaviour.

Private securities, today, trade at a discount to public securities, all or other things being equal, mainly because public securities are more "liquid". But as discussed in previous lessons, liquidity is not a characteristic intrinsic to a particular asset. It would seem that, by definition, the fact that they are public should be enough to prove that they are more liquid. However, it makes no sense to hold a public security to remain liquid, because there is already an institution called "money" that serves the purpose.

Conclusion

We have examined the relationship between the concept of decidability and capital structure. It is the undecided nature of entrepreneurship that makes any forecast on equity valuation a mere tautology. Human action cannot be formalized and we can therefore not value equity. What we call valuation is a tautological exercise. Obviously, this idea juxtaposes everything we have been told by value investors.

Two basic interventions seem critical: the development of limited liability and the establishment of legislation banning insider information. These interventions were exponentially enforced with the rise of democracies, as public markets make it easier to allocate the savings extracted through collective coercive pension contributions. The mutation of the concept of liquidity as explained before was also critical but not particularly targeted at this problem. The previous two interventions were enforced to favour the public equity market at the expense of the private equity. The subsidy on public equity is a hidden tax on innovation, as innovative entrepreneurs have to compete for funding against public companies, while the cost of going public has steadily grown over the years.[15] Without these interventions, public equity would trade at a discount to private equity.

Investors must not fall prey to these distortions. Once they establish their liquidity preference and know how much is available to invest (vis-à-vis their intertemporal preference), they can determine an approximate appetite for

---

[15] By subsidy here, I refer to the privilege that public equity enjoys over private, thanks to government intervention. I imagine that one would feel tempted to think too that limited liability in fact boosts innovation. It allows for mistakes to be made, entrepreneurs to try, fail and try again. This however assumes investors to be happy to risk their savings in the pursuit of those experiments, even more than with unlimited liability. This topic makes very well the subject of an entire, additional book. Personally, I believe that one is misled by the historical evidence in this regard. Correlation is not causation. Technological development was not facilitated by the rise of democracy and its institutions but ran parallel to and in spite of it. An example of this is Lavoisier's tragic end.

investing in equity. Within that space, and only after identifying investment (not trading) theses, investors must choose those who are the most undecidable. Preference should always be given to private ventures, where we can actively manage the inexorable uncertainty.

Bibliography

Johnston, David. (1995, June). Limiting Liability: Roman Law and the Civil Law Tradition. *Chicago-Kent Law Review*. Vol. 70, Issue 4. Symposium on Ancient Law, Economics & Society, Part I: The Development of Law in Classical and Early Medieval Europe. Article 6. Retrieved September 2016 from https://scholarship. kentlaw.iit.edu/cgi/viewcontent.cgi?article=2998&context=cklawreview

Malmendier, Ulrike. (n.d.). *Publicani*. Retrieved August 2016 from: https://eml. berkeley.edu/~ulrike/Papers/Publicani_Article_v5.pdf

Malmendier, Ulrike. (2008). *Law and Finance "at the Origin"*. Retrieved September 2016 from https://eml.berkeley.edu/~ulrike/Papers/JELDraft70.pdf

Grasselli, M. R., and Hurd, T. R. (McMaster University, Jan. 2010). *Credit Risk Modeling*. Hamilton, ON, Canada. Retrieved May 2015 from https://ms.mcmaster.ca/~grasselli/Credittext2011.pdf

Bank for International Settlements, Monetary and Economic Department. Developing corporate bond markets in Asia. *BIS Papers No 26: Proceedings of a BIS/PBC seminar held in Kunming, China on 17–18 November 2005*. Released February 2006 and retrieved May 2015 from https://www.bis.org/publ/bppdf/bispap26.pdf

Malmendier, Ulrike. (2002). *Societas Publicanorum, Staatliche Wirtschaftsactivitätenin den Händen privater Unternehmer*. Böhlau Verlag.

H. Grotius. (1583–1645). *De Iure belli ac pacis* 2.11.13. Digitized by the Internet Archive in 2008 with funding from Microsoft Corporation. Retrieved July 2015 from https://archive.org/details/hugonisgrottiide010grotuoft

Voet, Johannis. (1716). *Commentarius*, 14.1.5. European Libraries Collection, digitized by Google from the National Library of Naples. Retrieved July 2015 from https://ia800200.us.archive.org/10/items/bub_gb_ap8ZayGxPbwC/bub_gb_ap8ZayGxPbwC.pdf

Smith, Adam. (1776). *An Inquiry into the Nature and Causes of the Wealth of Nations. (Book V, Chapter I)*. Edinburgh: Thomas Nelson, 1843. Retrieved July 2015 via Google Books from: https://books.google.ca/books?id=8k_K8rf2fnUC&pg=PA5#v=onepage&q&f=false

5

Debt

It is no coincidence that the exponential growth of public capital markets took off after the creation of the Federal Reserve in 1913 and the expropriation of private money (i.e. gold) in the United States in 1933.[1] Democracy, public equity and inflation go hand in hand. Public equity and democracy need each other. The opposite is true for private debt. Nowhere was this made more evident than during the US Congressional hearings that took place in the winter of 1933, which preceded the expropriation of money. During a testimony before Congress, Marriner Eccles, who would later be Chairman of the Federal Reserve, made the following comments[2]:

> …*Money has no utility or economic value except to serve as a medium of exchange…* ( )…***Were it not for our debt structure, the fluctuating and unstable dollar would not raise such havoc with our economic system. Our debt and credit structure is the very foundation of our capitalistic society and our unstable dollar results in a large measure from the uncontrolled operation of this system.*** *The debt structure has obtained its present astronomical proportions due to an unbalanced distribution of wealth production as measured in buying power during our years of prosperity…*

For Eccles, debt, and more specifically the "debt structure" within a nation, was the obstacle to achieving the higher consumption levels that the government pursued through inflationary measures:

---

[1] Given the relevance of the United States at that time, this had a tremendous global impact.

[2] Investigations of Economic Problems, Hearings before the Committee on Finance, United States Senate, Seventy-Second Congress, Second Session, Pursuant to S. Res. 315, February 13 to 28, 1933.

© The Author(s) 2018
M. Arisson, *Investing in the Age of Democracy*,
https://doi.org/10.1007/978-3-319-95903-0_5

*...Several factors to-day stand in the way of increasing our money velocity. I repeat there is plenty of money today to bring about a restoration of prices, but the chief trouble is that it is in the wrong place; **it is concentrated** in the larger financial centers of the country, the **creditor sections**, leaving a great portion of the back country, or the debtor sections, drained dry and making it appear that there is a great shortage of money and that it is, therefore, necessary for the Government to print more...*

...During the period of the depression the creditor sections have acted on our system like a great suction pump, drawing a large portion of the available income and deposits in payment of interest, debts, insurance and dividends as well as in the transfer of balances by the larger corporations normally carried throughout the country. This makes for a shortage of funds in the agricultural areas and an excess of funds in the cities. During our period of prosperity funds were flowing from the creditor sections into the debtor sections in the extension of new credits and capital expansion as fast or faster than they were flowing out. There is no way of reviving the return flow through the operation of credit or investment until there is a basis for credit brought about through an increased price level and until there is an opportunity of profit through further investment of capital...

The exposition above shows the profound disgust of an interventionist administration for everything related to debt. I believe this was a relevant moment in the financial history of the United States and, if I may, of the world. There are in it, to begin with, a few misconceptions, like the notion of velocity of money[3] or that of debt structure, debt concentration or creditor/ debtor sections, which are outside the scope of this book, but they illustrate how an erroneous conceptual base leads to wrong conclusions. In the 1930s, during the gold exchange standard and the first decades of widespread central banking, policy makers in democratic nations began a systematic and method-ical approach against debt as a component of the capital structure, in general. Certainly, creditors had always been despised since the times of the pharaohs in Egypt. But until the 1930s, the fight had always taken a personal angle: It had been directed against bankers, or Jews or merchants. Never had debt itself been the target of criticism. Even under Canon Law, what had been put to the

---

[3] The concept of velocity of money is another aberration derived from thinking of money as an object instead of an institution. It was first formalized as part of the so-called Cambridge equation within the quantity theory of money. This equation states that there is a linear relationship between a demand for money, a fiction called "price level" and another platonic entity called "aggregate income" (in macro terms): $M = k * P * Y$, where k is a constant. Note how, for Eccles, a higher velocity of money is a desirable outcome. However, money can only serve its purpose when it is hoarded, which means that Eccles (and Keynesians in general) never understood what money is, confusing it with capital.

question was the payment of interest but not the funding of a venture by way of debt, let alone a discussion of the role of debt in an economic system.

Why would debt be despised? Debt is an explicit contract, with conditions, that requires above all, stability of cash flows from the debtor. Monetary and fiscal policies will always generate instability and, therefore, will affect those indebted. The "equitization" of liabilities is the act of converting a creditor into a forced investor, sharing the uncertainties associated with the debtor.[4] For a debtor in trouble, it is a way out of debt. In the 1930s, as a result of the imbalances created by the monetary policies of the Federal Reserve, the number of debtors in trouble, who had a vote, was overwhelming. And with it, the war against debt began and continues to this day.

Today, policy makers have shifted the focus of this war from the debt itself to the signals and mechanisms that define it. The main signal is the rate of interest, and as I write, it has been completely destroyed. I can say with confidence that in 2016–2017 and as a consequence of monetary policies initiated in 2009 nowhere in the planet does an interest rate provide any longer with a genuine and accurate signal to those in the savings and investments markets. Policy makers wrongly calculated that we would remain passive in the face of debt destruction. The markets proved them wrong. Since 2009, trading volumes in stock exchanges have all but shrunk, only partially offset by the rise of high-frequency trading. The introduction of negative rates and the current debate on the ban of cash are the last desperate attempts to deny this truth. Unfortunately, in the meantime, the generation of genuine savings has been negatively impacted and it is being reflected in the weak rates of growth exhibited globally.

Unlike public debt, private debt is without hesitation the most noble and oldest form of financing. For a creditor, if he is comfortable with the risk of default taken, debt increases his wealth by the mere passage of chronological time. It provides peace of mind and the ability to continue focusing on doing what he does best, without other worries. For a debtor, debt provides funding to his project, without losing control or the upside that he thinks the project will eventually bring.

As it is natural that more people will be willing to borrow savings than produce them, and because envy and the rule of the majority are the basis of democracy, it is also natural that those who end up being voted to rule will take a stand in favour of the majority who owe and against the few who save.

---

[4] For a good example, refer *Addressing the causes of low interest rates* May 2, 2016, by Mario Draghi, President of the European Central Bank. Draghi suggests that even under low-to-negative rates in 2016, savers can still earn satisfactory returns if they shift from debt to equity.

This has always been and will always be the case, which means that in times of democracy one will be deprived (in varying degrees) of accessing the most noble form of financing and investing. Democracy despises debt.

But, how noble is debt indeed? Figure 5.1 should provide an illustration. I show a hypothetical creation of wealth in real terms (i.e. adjusted for an arbitrary purchasing power index), for a period of 100 years, beginning in 1914. This period encompasses three generations. Assume that each of them works during a certain number of years, retires at 65 and passes out at 80. Therefore, in this case, the last generation inherits from the previous two. The graph presents three scenarios. In each of them, the annual income of each generation rises by 5% **on average**, due to productivity only, because it is reasonable to assume that as we progress in our lives, we earn more. As well, in the three scenarios, there is sovereign debt and I assume its benchmark ten-year rate is around 2% (a very, very generous assumption).

The **blue line** represents a case where there is **no inflation**. This is the way we used to save before the times of democracy, under the gold standard, say, between 1600 and 1780 in Amsterdam, or after 1815 and before World War I in the United Kingdom. During those times, governments did not coerce parents to have their children educated under an arbitrary and centrally planned curriculum; their education was diverse and empirical. They were allowed to enter the labour force early, as apprentices, which furnished them

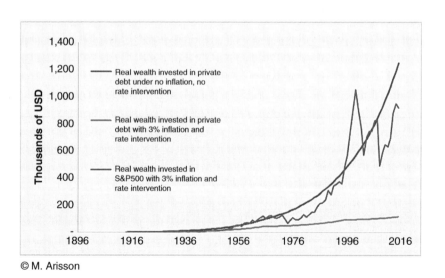

© M. Arisson

Fig. 5.1 Real wealth creation under different scenarios. (Color figure online)

with a trade.[5] Added no taxes on income or the use of labour,[6] the apprenticeship system guaranteed minimal unemployment.

Because there was no income tax, the three generations could have saved 15% of their annual income and invest it in private debt, relatively safe, at an annual interest rate of 4%, or 200 bps above sovereign.[7] In addition, due to productivity gains and lack of monetary policy, the purchasing power of money (i.e. gold) could rise 1% per year. It was a boring scenario, where citizens took care of their own savings and there were no coercive pension plans.

The **orange line** represents a case closer to what we experience nowadays: Money has been replaced by fiat currency and it is not too far-fetched to see a 3% annual drop in its purchasing power, on average. Income grows nominally only 1% per year, in addition to the 5% increase mentioned earlier, driven by productivity. In this case, I assume that the three generations still decide to invest their savings in corporate debt, based on tradition. However, central banks intervene in the interest rates market in this scenario, and the spread of private debt over sovereign is only 80 bps. Because citizens are forced to pay an income tax, I have assumed that the savings rate is not 15% as in the previous case but 10% (still, an extremely generous assumption) in light of the experience in the late twentieth century in developed countries.

The **grey line** represents a scenario where, because of the low performance of fixed income/credit, the generations decide to invest in public equity. In this case, public equity is represented by the S&P500 index. All other assumptions on purchasing power (−3%), nominal income growth (+1%) and savings rate (10%) remain unchanged.

Figure 5.1 shows the blue line (i.e. private debt at low and stable interest rate compounding) outperforming the other two strategies; yes, over a century, I know, but I look for perspective and in the developed countries, the

---

[5] The popular perception is that learning a trade was limiting and prevented a more general and diverse education. However, nothing is further from the truth. Unfortunately, one can only provide with inductive comparisons in this regard. I can think about the Wright brothers, who in their search for a flying machine, triggered research on aerodynamics, for instance. The particular astronomical interests of Sir Newton forced him to develop differential analysis, a tool. Today, the search for an efficient electrical car is forcing us to rethink the way we store and distribute energy. Lastly, my personal and tangible interest in protecting and growing my wealth has led me to write this book.

[6] In 2016, the European Union had no better idea than to level the field down, creating the legal figure of "electronic persons". If entrepreneurs will seek to avoid paying taxes on the use of labour by shifting to robots, robots will be taxed as well.

[7] This was not unusual within the British Empire, as related by Niall Ferguson in *The Ascent of Money*, Penguin Press, 2008: "…none of the sovereign or colonial bonds that traded in London in 1913 yielded more than two percentage points above consols…That meant that anyone who had bought a portfolio of foreign bonds, say, in 1880, had enjoyed handsome capital gains…". Note: "Consols" where short for "consolidated annuities". These were perpetual obligations issued by the Bank of England, first in 1751. They have been fully redeemed.

average life expectancy reaches eight decades (my two grandmothers lived healthy and way into their 90s). Not only does so decisively but also with considerably less volatility.

It underscores a scenario of general improvement of lifestyle where productivity increases and freedom to save and invest contributes to general progress. Because it takes place under no inflation, wealth is not redistributed and those who are in the lower percentiles of income benefit from an increase in the purchasing power of their wages and benefit from no devaluation of their hard-earned wealth. It was this environment, in the Netherlands of the seventeenth century, what allowed Europe to launch the Industrial Revolution, prior to the age of democracy. But this is a book about Finance and we will leave this discussion here. I only wanted to bring to your attention the merits of compounding in a stable and free environment where one can invest in private debt. In this context, it is clear that the longer the term horizon, the higher the final value of a dollar earned today, making it too precious to be wasted in public securities.

Labour

Before discussing the different forms of debt, I want to briefly mention the least recognized one: Labour. For those wannabe investors who lack savings, there is one alternative: To work for the company they would like to be able to invest in, but cannot afford to.

Employees actually advance resources to the entrepreneur, and in exchange, they receive a fixed sum of cash, in anticipation of the final product. This structure mimics that of a debt instrument. It is capped regardless of profits, if any. Workers thus renounce to the potential upside in profits that a company may eventually earn in exchange for the safety of a stable cash flow in advance (of the production process).

Once this formal equivalence between debt and labour (i.e. debt in kind) is appreciated, **it is easy to see why entrepreneurs can only hire more workers the more decidable their business model becomes**. Government intervention, on the other hand, in the form of labour legislation will only decrease such decidability and, therefore, affect the demand of labour. However, if a business model becomes more decidable, it will also be easier to replace labour with algorithms run by computers or machines.

Private Debt

Private debt is a contract between two parties that can also be collective (i.e. multiple borrowers or lenders). The difference with public debt, as I understand here, relies mainly on its transferability. Private debt cannot be transferred, traded, without the borrower's consent. With this definition, I am aware that I classify portions of syndicated bank debt, for instance, under the realm of public debt (Fig. 5.2).

		Does the loan trade?	
		Yes	No
Is the lending contract...	Direct (single lender)	N/A	Bilateral loan
	Collective (multiple lenders)	Syndicated loan	Private Placement

© M. Arisson

Fig. 5.2 Suggested debt categories

Because the parties deal directly with each other, the lender has the right to ask for direct access to all the relevant information on the decidability of the borrower's business model. Once the same is assessed, the structure of the loan, which is the most important, can be fleshed out. These three things must simultaneously exist in a loan contract: (a) Correct fit of the financial need at stake (i.e. borrowing cause), (b) encouragement to repay and (c) discouragement to default.

Borrowing Causes

Any borrower may need financing to support these five borrowing causes: (a) Working capital needs, (b) capital expenditures, (c) refinancing of other debt, (d) bridge to restructuring or (e) cash out (which can take place in other ways).

As a general rule, one must avoid lending for cashing out. Why would you want to put your money to earn interest in a business from which his owner wants to cash out? I am aware of the infinite reasons that can be provided to justify cashing out. None has ever convinced me, personally. If a business has good prospects, there is no reason to cash out.[8]

---

[8] Unfortunately, this borrowing cause has increased since the crisis of 2008. It is only natural, considering that under Quantitative Easing, any business with access to funding at very low rates becomes an instantaneous ATM.

However, should one still decide to lend under this cause, one must ensure that from a structural perspective, as a lender, one will have easy and quick access to control of the company, should its financial condition deteriorate. This means that unless provisions for collateralization (if not right from the start) are taken with appropriate financial covenants, a lender will be unable to limit whatever potential damage the cash out transaction unleashed.

A bridge (to restructuring) loan, from previous comments, should be understood as a trade, not as an investment. In this type of loans, the exit strategy is key. Each case is unique as the market appetite for each restructuring changes with time and context. Most of these loans include step-up pricing (i.e. pricing that increases with time to encourage the borrower to conclude the transaction that is being bridged) and an upfront fee. When bridge loans are bilateral (i.e. not syndicated), the lender generally (although not necessarily) acts as adviser too. One way to discern whether the exit strategy is solid is to examine how decidable the new business model will be and to contrast it against the target capital structure (i.e. post-bridge). For instance, if a loan will bridge a spin-off to a new bulk shipping company and the exit strategy is to take said loan out via the equity market (i.e. raising equity), under normal macroeconomic conditions, one should hesitate. Bulk shipping is fairly decidable: Its business model can be formalized ex ante, within a recursive[9] set of basic equations (i.e. value drivers). A prospective investor in the spin-off may not want to participate in an equity transaction, because he would be subject to a future bond issuance where the stability of income is passed through to bondholders, while he, as an equity holder, is left to bear the burden of the bulk shipping market risk. The equity issue will probably succeed only at a discount.

In debt refinancing, one cannot anticipate a specific common theme to look for. Perhaps the one that interests me most is how the transaction stands relative to others under similar conditions. Ideally, one would have a benchmark from the same borrower. But this cannot be the case under private, bilateral debt transactions. If it was, the borrower would not be dealing bilaterally, but accessing the public debt market. The new debt will by necessity finance a previous transaction, which to me is a signal that an amortization schedule should be in place. Eventually, it is important to see that the borrower is willing to pay the debt off, rather than refinance it.

The aforementioned borrowing causes are usually addressed with term loans. For working capital or capital expenditures needs, a revolving loan is more appropriate. Once more, when financing capital expenditures, it is important to look into the nature of the business being financed. (Oil/gas)

---

[9] Refer Lesson 3: "Turing's decidability in Finance".

reserve-based lending in the US and Canadian shale areas during the 2010–2014 period was a tool to finance with debt business models that were not that decidable. It was not clear how the identified oil and gas reserves were going to be extracted and at what final cost. There were competing technologies in a sector that in the past, in the absence of monetary interventions, was the perfect candidate for venture capital. What made things worse is that the debt financing was carried out by institutions that practise fractional reserve lending, linking its demise with systemic risk.[10]

Repayment

There are basically two ways to encourage repayment. The first one consists in establishing, according to each case's needs, a series of covenants that either allocate a portion of generated cash for repayment or constrain any unexpected move away from the general business model. The second way is simply to design an amortization structure that matches the operations cycle being financed. Hence, the importance of understanding the decidability of the borrower's business model. In any case, the intelligent lender will have a minimum repayment structure design included in the bilateral contract. So-called covenant-lite structures are nothing short of an accident waiting to happen.

Lastly, tenor is also relevant. The maturity of a loan has to have a natural fit with the borrowing cause and borrower's operating cycle. For instance, to extend a seven-year term loan B (i.e. to institutional investors, with very little amortization) to a borrower in a sector as dynamic as media and telecommunications is irresponsible in my view. For this sector, seven years is an eternity, as new technologies and production processes may leave the borrower's business obsolete.

Discouragement to Default

Under this classification, one can think of dissuading, of punitive options, to discourage default. These are last-resort options and in no way do they ever compensate for bad structuring of the two previous factors (i.e. borrowing causes and repayment). They are simple remedies. The most common one is (over)collateralization of the debt: the contractual obligation of the borrower to release pledged property in favour of the lender if default occurs. But there are others, which also work while the obligation is still on. For instance, one

[10] The Bank of Canada was forced to depreciate the Canadian dollar, by maintaining low its benchmark rate.

should always ensure that one's debt matures before that of other lenders, if any, or before a relevant event that could impact negatively on the borrower's behaviour towards his duty to repay.

Bilateral Loans

Bilateral loans are democracy's most despised form of financing. They represent diversity, institutional innovation, two parties contracting freely and acknowledging mutual property rights, choosing jurisdictions to settle their disputes. In other words, bilateral loans explicit freedom. For those who manage pools of savings or for regulators, this same diverse nature means higher allocation costs. These groups will therefore not promote bilateral loans, at best. **However, this type of loans is the best savings vehicle an individual can have.** I have personally observed the irony that in nations which suffered high inflation, because the banking industry could not develop, bilateral loans (in foreign currency and secured) were left to the average citizen to make and thus became an impressive savings tool. This is one of the counterintuitive reasons why in these nations, where average incomes are definitely low, average citizens manage to save important figures, while the average Joe in a developed country is insolvent, mortgaged up to his neck and lives paycheck to paycheck. The citizen of the suffered nation is encouraged to save because saving pays off: He can entrepreneurially discover the interest rate, the structure of the loan and satisfy himself with tailored security packages, from his friendly (and relatively inexpensive) law firm.

Bilateral loans tend to have short maturities, seldom beyond three years. While under syndicated loans borrowers are generally bound to financial covenants, bilateral loans usually lack them. This characteristic is offset by solid security packages but, in my opinion, investors should always aim for the former.

Private Placements

Private placements are a hybrid category between what I called private debt and public debt. A private placement is still not traded publicly in a market but is no longer a direct lending contract between two parties. The lenders are usually institutional investors, the loan does not amortize and its tenor is beyond five years. Private placements can be senior or subordinated to other obligations.

With these characteristics, investors should only buy these obligations if they finance a decidable business model, with long-term prospects.

At origination, private placements can be split in units of equal book value. These placements are the main alternative of debt financing vis-à-vis a SEC-registered offering, avoiding registration under the Securities Act of 1933, reporting under the Securities Act of 1934. Because these placements are not offered to the general public, there is often no need for the issuers to provide detailed financial reports or a prospectus.

Syndicated Loans

When a potential lending commitment to a borrower would breach the exposure limits self-imposed by a bank, the bank forms a syndicate with other institutions to share in said commitment, thus reducing their exposure to a level they can tolerate. The loans that are therefore shared among banks are called syndicated loans.[11] These loans are structured, arranged and administered by one or some of the lenders.

Syndicated loans are found in both the investment grade and leveraged loan markets, and their growth has been mostly driven by leveraged buyouts. The syndicated loan market is not for the retail but for the institutional investor. Some control in the lending process is retained, as the covenants (financial, negative and affirmative) of their respective credit agreements typically demand that at least 51% of the syndicate banks approve their amendments.

Corporate Bonds

Among all debt securities, corporate bonds are the ones that give us the least amount of control on our debt investments. They are subordinated to secured debt and usually mature after pari-passu bank unsecured debt or private placements. Issuers usually have the option to call corporate bonds if the relevant interest rates fall after their issuance. The exposure to insiders cannot be ignored. However, if we invest in corporate bonds from an asset class perspective, through an index (but not a leveraged or structured one), we may minimize this exposure.

When I have to invest in corporate bonds, the decidability aspect of the issuer's business model is my main criteria. If I can make sense of a bond from this perspective, execution is straightforward.

---

[11] When the number of participating banks is lower than seven, the loans are also called club loans.

Bibliography

Investigations of Economic Problems, Hearings before the Committee on Finance, United States Senate, Seventy-Second Congress, Second Session, Pursuant to S. Res. 315, February 13 to 28, 1933.

Von Mises, Ludwig. (1949). *Human Action: A Treatise on Economics*. Auburn, AL: Ludwig von Mises Institute, Scholar's Edition, 1998.

Draghi, Mario, President of the European Central Bank. (2016). *Addressing the causes of low interest rates*. Introductory speech held at a panel on "*The future of financial markets: A changing view of Asia*" at the Annual Meeting of the Asian Development Bank, Frankfurt am Main, 2 May 2016. Retrieved May 2016, from https://www.ecb.europa.eu/press/key/date/2016/html/sp160502.en.html

6

Institutions

The word "market" usually denotes a physical place, a venue, where business is conducted. That is a typical representation. But a market is a process; a process of social coordination. And all coordination processes rely on protocols, rules or let's call them "standards". When it comes to social coordination, such protocols are what we generally understand (and Roman jurists understood) by institutions. Institutions allow social coordination to succeed. Yet, they are most underrated and least understood, perhaps because they grow out of spontaneous, unplanned, trial-and-error processes that are constantly evolving. Why do they evolve and do so constantly? Because uncertainty, the kinds of which cannot be computed, is omnipresent in our lives.

When these protocols prove themselves useful over time and end up shaping our behaviour, we can identify them as legal institutions. **They capture the ontological nature of the "non-computable" problem that they first set themselves to address.** One of the oldest institutions that survive to this day is family. Probably the reason it has survived for so long has to do with the fact that the institution also addresses the uncertainties related to ageing. As humans lengthened their life expectancy, and as long as reading and writing were exceptional, we realized that availing ourselves with a wealth of experience possessed by our elders was valuable and, in exchange, we learned to take care of them (back then, our old were not so old and the caring might have not been intensive) under a common roof. It is no coincidence that in present times, the institution of family has suffered most in those nations where governments imposed public education and public pension plans.

© The Author(s) 2018
M. Arisson, *Investing in the Age of Democracy*,
https://doi.org/10.1007/978-3-319-95903-0_6

Institutions permeate our lives. They are so ingrained that we barely notice them. Clothing, for instance, is an institution. Luxury goods too.[1] However, the two most important and perennial institutions are money and language, with money being more important than language, as Dr Huerta de Soto correctly points out. As soon as humans realized that trading was efficient, the uncertainties embedded in barter, which is the most primitive form of trade, were addressed with the institution of money, which over thousands of years of evolution culminated in the adoption of gold.

Language too is constantly evolving. Like most fundamental institutions, language is the result of an anarchic, continuous and spontaneous coordination process. Its evolution depends on how fluid the process is: When humans are able to trade thanks to a sound and healthy medium of indirect exchange, they are compelled to communicate. The more competitive the business environment is within a free market, the more refined and more widely used our language has to be to succeed entrepreneurially. This explains the expansion of Latin and English beyond their respective original demographics, while simultaneously achieving refinement. The works of Virgil or Shakespeare or Cervantes illustrate this point. The opposite is also valid: As soon as the Roman Empire suffered inflation, leading to the extinction of commerce across the Empire, Latin degenerated into regional dialects. The same could be true for the English language, if the United States is eventually unable to finance its navy in the Pacific Ocean and the safety of transpacific commerce is put at risk.

The success and survival of institutions depend on how well adapted and flexible they are to the needs (to address uncertainty) they satisfy. I shall refer to this characteristic as the ontological nature of institutions.

Because institutions address uncertainty, it is not possible to describe them formally. Their ontological nature explains why mathematical economic models have no place for institutional analysis. Mathematics is recursive. Decidability belongs to finite spaces, not infinite ones. And this is the case even under Quantum Algebra.[2] Such an ex ante definition is foreign to creativity and abstraction proper of any entrepreneurial act.

With this brief and in no way fair general introduction to institutions, I shall now concentrate on those private institutions that are essential to the investing process: The irregular deposit, the loan, money and banking. Smart investors understand and correctly discriminate them.

---

[1] There is nothing physically intrinsic to a luxury good. We demand luxury goods not because of their quality but simply because we know only a few can afford them. Owning them sets us socially apart. Luxury goods are therefore an institution, a temporal category.

[2] Operations using bra-ket notation require that we define a specific space ex ante.

Private Institutions

The Irregular Deposit[3]

The institution of deposit[4] addresses an eternal need: to safe keep something valuable. This need was recognized from times immemorial and Rome had extensive jurisprudence dealing with it. When the goods deposited were fungible, Roman juris consults referred to the respective deposit contracts as "irregular". Under irregular deposits, the custodian of the deposited good was responsible for keeping the good and returning the equivalent in both quantity and quality. In their words, the custodian had to guarantee the *tantundem*.[5] The irregular deposit contract was the original contract in the business of banking, and it is well documented that it was breached early in history.

The defining feature of this institution is that a demand on the deposit can be exercised at any time and without prior notice.[6] If the custodian has to return the equivalent quantity and quality at any time it is requested by the depositor, he deserves a compensation for the service provided. If today custodians remunerate depositors, it is because the concept of deposit has been completely corrupted. Indeed, there is ample evidence that in Ancient Greece and Rome bankers failed to keep custody of the amounts deposited to them. But when they did, their dealings were identified as a crime. No one challenged the institution of irregular deposit itself. This state of affairs would remain so until the Middle Ages, when the Church forbade charging interest on loans (we deal with the loan institution further below) and it became imperative to disguise loans as deposits. This type of loan, disguised as a deposit, was called *depositum confessatum* (singular). It was termed *confessatum* because the custodian "confessed" that he was accepting money in deposit,

---

[3] These comments are based on Huerta de Soto, *Money, Bank Credit and Economic Cycles, 3rd English Edition, 2012.* I encourage the interested reader to refer to this monumental work.

[4] The word deposit comes from Latin: De – Posit, to remove, to dislodge oneself from something.

[5] *Tantundem eiusdem generis, qualitatis et bonetatis.*

[6] As Dr Huerta de Soto points out, this ontological characteristic of the deposit institution means that an American call option and a repo contract are also deposit contracts. At any time, either the buyer of the American call option or the buyer of the repo contract has the right to demand the call's exercise or the repurchase clause. This means that at any time, the seller of the call option and the seller of the repo must be able to honour their obligation, in an equivalent quantity and quality. In the case of a repo contract, this characteristic is what makes repo financing, also known as shadow banking, so dangerous to the current financial system. Central bankers and regulators know this, as well as the fact that the funding market is arbitraged, because repo funding is not subject to the same rules that limit fiat currency funding (for banks). Banks, in aggregate, can only lever deposits about nine to ten times, while no limits are imposed to repo funding. In 2017, one can only hope that regulators will keep this institutional aspect of the repo market in mind, when they replace LIBOR (i.e. unsecured lending benchmark rate, probably by 2022) with the Broad Treasuries Financing Rate (BTFR).

rather than taking a loan. The catch was that at maturity, it would be noted that the depositor had requested the amount deposited back and, because it was not available, the custodian would pay a fine to the depositor, who would then simultaneously renew the deposit contract. That fine, de facto, was the interest paid on the loan. Since then and to this date, loans are confused with deposits.

The Loan

Another relevant institution is the loan. A loan is a protocol to address the need to trade intertemporal preferences between lenders and borrowers. A loan therefore is an exchange contract between those to whom (marginal) present consumption is worth less than future consumption, and others who either value present consumption more or can put the transferred savings to use into a venture. The characteristic that the demand of a loan can only be effected after a certain period (i.e. at maturity) is fundamental to this institution. And because of it, is compensated by the loan interest rate.

Just as important as the role played by institutions is the impact that innovation has had on them. Because "good" institutions can only proceed from unplanned, spontaneous trial-and-error experiments, whenever innovation is either imposed or planned, attention must be paid. **It is often those traders who understand this point who are the most successful. Because by identifying failed institutions, they can bet against them in epic trades.** One example of a failed institution was Argentina's convertible monetary system, imposed by law in 1991, which simultaneously allowed the existence of fractional reserve banking for US dollar-denominated local deposits. Another one, which will sooner or later come to light, is the coexistence of the Basel III regulatory framework with the collateralization of assets, also known as shadow banking. In many ways, in the twenty-first century and under the current levels of financial repression, the only way to make money is to arbitrage the governments' interventions on private institutions.

Money

I will refer to money only insofar as it relates to investing. I will therefore not provide a thorough study of money. Money is an institution. It is not a tangible object. However, we constantly identify this institution with one. We have to, because it is ontological to the institution of money the need of tangible, movable, and redeemable materialization of purchasing power.[7] But just as we are constantly identifying money with an object, we are also simultaneously always, consciously or not, seeking to improve that association with any other object that better fits our need for money. Over thousands of years, this search for the best object materialized in gold. It does not mean however that the search is finished. But gold met the features required by that protocol, that institution, called money. These are scarcity, fungibility or homogeneity, ease of mobility or redeemability and the absence of counterparty risk.

To be a good store of value, the institution of money must be materialized into a scarce object. The scarcer the object, the more efficiently it works as money. When the object is homogeneous, there can be no arbitrage, nor can money be doubted in its usefulness. Fungibility is critical for the development of capital markets. When the object serving as money is fungible, financial intermediation can exist. I elaborate more on this topic later in this lesson. Money can only work if it is easy to move or redeem so that we can protect the value stored in it.

As Ludwig von Mises rightly said, the history of money is nothing else but the history of government's attempts to destroy it. Since 1971 and for all practical purposes, money has been nationalized through confiscation. The nationalization was a slow but steady process that began in May 1933, triggered by a run on the entire gold exchange standard system that started in 1931, with the fall of the KreditAnstalt in Wien. The nationalization of money is a recurrent theme in democracies. In Sparta, gold and silver were confiscated under Lycurgus[8] and replaced with iron coins. The French and American revolutions were also exposed to similar experiences, with France living the most dramatic one, with the assignats. It ended in hyperinflation.

Since 1971, we have been deprived of money and forced to use credit instead, also known as fiat money. Fiat money, as we know today, meets some of the features we attribute to money, but lacks two fundamental ones: The

---

[7] Redeemability and, for now, fungibility are absent in virtual currencies.

[8] "…*he resolved to make a division of their movables too, that there might be no odious distinction or inequality left amongst them; but finding that it would be very dangerous to go about it openly, he took another course, and defeated their avarice by the following stratagem: he commanded that all gold and silver coin should be called in, and that only a sort of money made of iron should be current, a great weight and quantity of which was very little worth; so that to lay up twenty or thirty pounds there was required a pretty large closet, and, to remove it, nothing less than a yoke of oxen. With the diffusion of this money, at once a number of vices were banished from Lacedaemon; for who would rob another of such a coin? Who would unjustly detain or take by force, or accept as a bribe, a thing which it was not easy to hide, nor a credit to have, nor indeed of any use to cut in pieces? For when it was just red hot, they quenched it in vinegar, and by that means spoilt it, and made it almost incapable of being worked…*". Lycurgus, Plutarch, 75 AC (trans. John Dryden, in www.http://classics.mit.edu/Plutarch/lycurgus.html).

absence of counterparty risk and scarcity. It has therefore ceased to be storage of value to remain a simple legal (i.e. by coercion) tender for indirect exchange.

Because gold is money, gold is not an investment asset. Neither is foreign exchange. These are assets to satisfy liquidity preference. **In general, one can think of currency trading themes as simple arbitrage between the relative qualities of money attributes.** Usually, the predominant arbitraged feature is scarcity: We buy the scarce money and sell the abundant one. But there is also arbitrage on the other attributes.[9] A run against a bank can be thought in terms of an arbitrage on redeemability. Soon in democracies, cash versus electronic money will be a case of arbitrage of fungibility, to avoid control from governments. When bills are finally taken out of circulation, the institution of money will have to be secured under a different vehicle, and deposits at a bank will not be considered money, but trapped and taxable purchasing power. The arbitrage will therefore shift from a qualitative aspect to a jurisdictional one, so that individuals can hold bills from governments that do not outlaw cash. I venture to say that this jurisdictional arbitrage may be so painful for democracies that can even be cause for war against the nation that refuses to ban cash.

Gold

Gold is money.[10] It is not a capital asset. It does not produce income. When you buy gold, you do not invest your savings. You simply change fiat currency (i.e. credit) for money.

Gold is money as a result of a spontaneous process of social coordination that developed throughout thousands of years. Its physical qualities, ease of transportation and scarcity satisfied the ontological nature of money like no other commodity could. If the history of money is the history of governments' attempts to destroy it, the history of money is the history of governments' attempts to control, seize and debase gold. And since 1971, it is also the history of governments' attempts to intervene the gold market.

Since the French Revolution (i.e. 1789), democracy has expanded relentlessly, worldwide. Under democracy, rulers govern because they obtain the popular vote. Rulers owe allegiance to voters, and to show it, they are tempted to either redistribute wealth (from minorities to majorities) or create inflation. This puts a democratic ruler in direct conflict with those who seek to protect

---

[9] In 2016, the trade between Bitcoin and the Chinese yuan was an arbitrage on redeemability… and privacy.

[10] But money is not gold. This is not a bijective relationship.

the purchasing power of their savings stored in gold. In this sense, gold is not only money but also insurance against the collapse of democracies caused by loss of control (by central banks; I elaborate more on this scenario, in Lesson 8). Because this loss of control is inexorable and the natural outcome of interventions, one feels compelled to own gold at all times, in a proportion according to one's subjective assessment of the health of central banking.

Intervention of the Gold Market

A popular idea is that gold is a good hedge against inflation. In its simplest form, gold cannot be printed, and as its relative scarcity against that of fiat money slowly increases, its price should spike. The implicit formula behind this idea can be represented as follows (Fig. 6.1):

Given a constant demand for money…

$$\frac{1\ \text{USD}}{1\ \text{Au oz}} = f\left(\frac{\text{Monetary base \textbf{usd} x Credit multiplier \textbf{usd} (includes shadow banking)}}{\text{Stock of Au ounces outstanding}}\right)$$

Fig. 6.1 Price determination of gold (in ounces), in USD, without intervention

The above relationship shows the price of gold in terms of a fiat currency (in this case, the US dollar) as a function of the relative supplies of gold and the US dollar. In the case of a fiat currency, its supply is the product of two factors: the monetary base created by the respective central bank and the corresponding credit multiplier. This multiplier reflects every single mean by which the original base is expanded, through the banking system and the shadow banking system.

If the relationship above was indeed representative of the state of affairs we're in, there would be no room for intervention. The supply of gold, in terms of ounces available, could be perhaps capped or confiscated, but not expanded. The rise in the price of gold, therefore, could not be suppressed.

To suppress it, however, central banks recur to new currency: Fiat gold. Given a constant demand for money, the formula involved now is (Fig. 6.2):

$$\frac{1\ \text{USD}}{1\ \text{Au oz}} = f\left(\frac{\text{Monetary base \textbf{usd} x Credit multiplier \textbf{usd} (includes shadow banking)}}{\text{Stock of Au ounces outstanding x Credit multiplier \textbf{Au}}}\right)$$

Fig. 6.2 Price determination of gold, in USD, with intervention

As you can see from the second relationship above, the genius of central banks was not to forbid gold but to morph it into another fiat currency by adding a credit multiplier to it. With this, it only takes to proportionally expand this credit multiplier as fast as necessary to make the price of gold fall regardless of fundamentals.

Below, I present the steps involved in the expansion of the supply of fiat gold (Fig. 6.3).

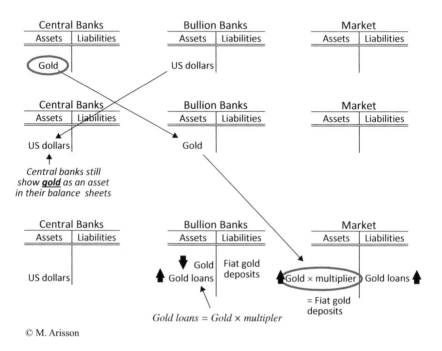

© M. Arisson

Fig. 6.3 How central banks create fiat gold ex nihilo

The above graph shows the aggregate balance sheets of the central banks, intermediaries and the gold market. Intermediaries handle transactions in precious metals and, in this case, in gold. As you can see, central banks hold gold as part of their assets. However, they can swap their gold holdings for liquidity, for US dollars. This swap is a mere exchange and is shown as step one, in the graph. Central banks sustain that these swaps are for temporary liquidity management purposes because they remove US dollars from the market (i.e. from the intermediaries). At a later date, not shown in the graph, the intermediaries should return the gold to the central banks, and receive US dollars back (including an interest). For this reason, because the swap contract implies the return of the gold at a later stage, central banks defend that they can continue showing the gold they swapped in their balance sheets as their asset. Once the physical gold is in the hands (i.e. balance sheet) of the inter-mediaries, these can create loans against it, supplying the market with fiat gold. This is shown in step two. Gold is debited and gold loans are credited. The ultimate amount of gold loans outstanding is a factor of the credit multi-plier in fiat gold. The higher the multiplier, the higher the supply of fiat gold in the market and the pressure on the price to drop.

How far can central banks go with this intervention? How long can it last? Is there a mechanism by which the market should revert to fundamentals? The answer is that central banks can go very, very far, and the intervention can last longer than you or I am willing to believe because the credit multiplier in fiat gold is not disclosed.[11] The public that holds physical gold or the central banks that accumulate physical gold but do not enter into swaps with them cannot force a contraction in the credit multiplier. By their actions (i.e. hoarding of physical gold), all they can do is to force the rest of the central banks and inter-mediaries to take a higher risk in the expansion of the multiplier. But they can-not force a rush for delivery. They are, by definition, outside of the system.

Banking and Financial Intermediation

Given the purposeful confusion between deposits and loans, it was only natu-ral that the activity of banking would get discredited. Lending that which was deposited in custody is one thing. To lend it multiple times over is another. And that is actually what has taken place over centuries. The modus operandi is called fractional reserve banking, and it could well have started as a means for bankers to avoid getting caught with gold by rulers in need of funds.

Those who defend fractional reserve banking argue that its associated cyclical financial crashes are the product of greed and imprudence by bankers and that proper regulatory frameworks based on probability theory are the basis for sound banking. If this is correct, after Basel III we should have shut central banks alto-gether. Not only did we not, but also less than a decade after the last financial crisis of 2008, an event as simple as the drop in the price of oil in 2015 triggered massive equity losses for banks globally. Why is therefore this view incorrect? We hold money because we live under uncertainty, unable to address it with proba-bility theory. We have learned to deal with uncertainty by creating the institu-tion of money. And because a demand deposit should be as good as money, depositors treat it as such. They rely on their deposits to address uncertainty. We don't know where or when the shots are going to come from! But we sure know that they will come. Hence, we keep some of our savings in the form of money.

---

[11] Banking in any fiat currency is regulated by strict disclosure requirements regarding capital, leverage and liquidity. Gold banking is not.

As we saw earlier, probability theory deals with mass, collective phenomena, which exhibit a determined frequency and a convergence, regardless of randomness in our observations. Our economic decisions are unique and do not belong to collective phenomena. They converge to nothing in particular nor can anyone say that they exhibit a frequency or much less that if a hint of frequent behaviour is spotted, said behaviour would pass the test of randomness. Regardless of the quality of our statistical analysis or the computing power of our technology or the prudence of bankers when they make their lending decisions, the fact is that the misappropriation and simultaneous conversion of a demand deposit into a loan can only end in an imbalance and panic. The time it takes for this process to materialize is irrelevant.

Nevertheless, banks do perform the important role of financial intermediation. Borrowing and lending are information-seeking and information-producing activities vital to social coordination. If we ignore the role of entrepreneurship and assume either perfect information or "given" information, our view on financial intermediation can only be dismissive. It is precisely this view what lies behind blockchain technology, which in turn, supports Bitcoin.

Lending is a skill. First, one needs to understand the market a prospective borrower is in and how the future capital structure will fit the financial operations associated with his business model. The credit agreement has to capture and reflect the reality observed while at the same time discourage default. Borrowing savings or interbank lending involves continuous active participation in shaping institutions, processes and behaviours required to channel savings from different players to different sectors and parts of the capital structure. Because these are constantly changing, this participation is dynamic. It is a learning process. The more regulated the interbank market is, the slower the learning becomes. As banks borrow and lend, they provide an indispensable transmission channel for savings to fund investments in an efficient and scalable way.

Virtual Currencies

The evolution of scientism since the eighteenth century and computing science in the past one, together with the ignorance of the most basic economic concepts (i.e. the concept of money), gave us virtual currencies in the twenty-first century. In the following paragraphs, I will limit myself to examine their nature and whether or not they are consistent with the institution of money:

A virtual currency, by definition, is not redeemable. Because of this, the first and ultimate way to establish ownership rights on it is with accounting entries. This means that a virtual currency, so far, is also not fungible. No one can carry a virtual currency in his wallet (at least not in a physical wallet). A system where property over virtual currency balances is established with accounting entries can be either centralized (with a master ledger) or distributed. Driven partly by a misunderstanding of the role of banks as financial mediators, and partly by utopia, Bitcoin was developed as a distributed system, based on blockchain technology.

The blockchain is a distributed database, but precisely because of this distributed structure and its non-fungible nature, lending appears to be possible only under a so-called peer-to-peer framework. This means that intermediation through a financial institution is not efficient in Bitcoin. Without fungibility, the amount of calculations a financial institution would have to carry could grow exponentially with each transaction. Perhaps the development of quantum computing will be able to overcome this obstacle, but in the meantime, the Bitcoin banks in existence are simply custodian banks. They do not lend nor borrow.

But let's assume that a new technology overcame the calculations costs associated with blockchain technology, making virtual currencies fungible. In this scenario, fractional reserve banking would be feasible, launching a credit expansion with an unchecked credit multiplier. Because virtual currencies are not redeemable, there would be no bank runs. Banks would have a free ticket to devalue steadily, defeating the purpose of virtual currencies. This is the same goal that in 2016 drives central banks to eliminate cash: To exert a steady and inescapable devaluation on our fiat currency holdings.

Now, if Bitcoin became fungible and Bitcoin banks were regulated, given that Bitcoin would still not be redeemable, these banks would be at a disadvantage vis-à-vis fiat money (assuming cash remains legal in the future) banks. In other words, I find it hard to see serious competition from virtual currencies. Bitcoin in its current state is not money but a conduit for capital to escape dangerous jurisdictions. Other assets played this role before (i.e. ADRs or traveller's cheques in Argentina in 2001).

Innovation in Institutions

I cannot end these comments without reminding myself that institutions are not set in stone. They are dynamic and change, as long as the reality that they seek to capture changes too. However, certain features which are inherent to social cooperation have a few eternal elements. Intertemporal preference is one of them, and we have learned to develop coordinated behaviour around it:

To encourage, channel and measure savings, for instance. Any time an institution that genuinely solves our ontological needs is mutated, we must pause, doubt and examine the proposed change. For its blind acceptance carries unforeseen consequences of the broadest impact. This is not to say one must oppose or ignore them, but to simply examine them beforehand. Since 2009, the de facto destruction of interest rates by central banks has led investors to abandon the institution of debt and replace it with dividend-paying stocks. In the long term, this innovation does not address the ontological nature of the investors or of those companies with undecidable business models that pay dividends to boost the price of their equity. The resolution of this incompatibility, when it finally takes place, will be painful.

Public Institutions

Public institutions are the protocols that coordinate action between governments and citizens, as well as among governments. Given the considerable diversity of constitutions and forms of governments across geographies and at different times, it would take an entire book to address their respective institutions. The point I want to make here, however, is that we cannot ignore them because they have a significant impact on the capital markets.

Consider this anecdote: in 2010, Martin Redrado, then President of the Banco Central de la República Argentina, was interviewed. Redrado had gained public attention after he refused to hand over USD 6.6 billion in reserves to the Treasury of Argentina to service upcoming debt maturities. He was forced to resign by then President Néstor Kirchner. At a later interview, Redrado was asked why he thought the Treasury should not use the so-called excess reserves of the central bank (to repay fiscal debt) if the amount of reserves was at the time higher than the monetary base in pesos. He answered that the question denoted misapprehension and added that in 1989, when Argentina had hyperinflation, the amount of reserves was actually higher than the amount of "currency in circulation". Redrado continued to point that the relevant metric a central bank should follow is not "Demand for currency", but the *potential* demand for currency. He explained that under **institutional uncertainty,** Argentines might not renew term deposits at maturity (a component of M2). As these term deposits mature, they become demand deposits, which people then convert into US dollars. Therefore, the Banco Central has to maintain a level of reserves that will guarantee enough supply, to a **potential** demand of US dollars, and term deposits cannot be ignored. Redrado understood his institutional context. He had called it: Argentina had no such thing as "excess reserves".

Another case of institutional negligence, this time more relevant, is represented by the Eurozone crisis. When it started in 2010 and for a long time after, popular wisdom held that it was a simple liquidity event.[12] I, however, sustained all along that the Eurozone crisis was caused by institutional failure and incompatibility. Policy makers and analysts reasoned that because peripheral euro sovereigns have their debt denominated in euros, all we needed was liquidity support. But every currency crisis is the consequence of an assessment made by its holders that their currency no longer can serve both to transact and to store value. The reason is always institutional. It doesn't matter what the trade or fiscal deficits are (the US dollar is the best example) or what a government's financing need is. At the heart of a currency crisis you have a crisis of confidence. Currency holders ask themselves: "Will we be 'taxed' for holding pesos, or euros?"

But the Eurozone peripheral countries were (and still are) not facing a liquidity crisis. The issue was and is far more serious. The whole European Union still faces an institutional crisis. Will the Eurozone behave as a Confederation or as a Union? The cost of not standing up to the circumstance and showing a firm resolution will eventually be far more expensive than higher borrowing costs. The European Central Bank must not believe for a second that what is at stake is a "liquidity problem of peripherals". Extrapolating Redrado's comments, the European Central Bank must understand that in these peripherals there is also a *potential* demand for a reserve currency that will be triggered violently without notice if the Eurozone acts as a Confederation, rather than a Union. In this case, liquidity support lines will be useless and will only delay a horrible end. What institution does the Eurozone lack? A unified bond market.

The institutional wary investor asks the following question: If the European Union is actually not a Union, but a Confederation, why should euros be held as the world's alternative reserve currency, instead of Canadian dollars or Australian dollars or Swiss francs? It is a valid question and a question markets are still asking in 2017.[13]

---

[12] "Default (even a sovereign one) is a liquidity Event", Jeffrey Rosenberg, "*US Fixed Income Situation*", Fixed Income Strategy, February 5, 2010, Bank of America.

[13] H. Sanguinetti, *Curso de Derecho Político*, 4th Edition, 2000, (my translation): *Confederations are alliances of sovereign states. In a Confederation, the links among members are weaker. The legal instrument of the alliance is a "treaty". The purpose of a Confederation is economic integration and military assistance among members. Member states remain sovereign and as such, keep the powers of self-determination. Confederated states reserve the right to nullify, reject legislation and, eventually, of secession. They may issue currency, keep customs and sustain armed forces. They lack a strong common government, although they may unify their foreign policy. In a Union, the links among member states are more vigorous. In a Union, one finds a definitive purpose to integrate the states. There is a sovereign federal government, while the states are autonomous. The states can govern themselves, have their own legislation, but these acts are subordinated to the Union's constitution and federal laws. Secession is not allowed, although member states conserve those rights that they did not delegate to the federal government, when the Union was established.*

Bibliography

Plutarch. (75 A.C.E.). *Lycurgus.* Translated by John Dryden. Retrieved May 2015 via The Internet Classics Archive from http://classics.mit.edu/Plutarch/lycurgus.html

Rosenberg, Jeffrey. (2010, February 5). Default (even a sovereign one) is a liquidity Event. *US Fixed Income Situation, Fixed Income Strategy.* Bank of America.

Sanguinetti, Horacio. (1986). *Curso de Derecho Político.* Buenos Aires: Editorial Astrea, 4ta Edición, 2000.

Part III

Economic Concepts

7

Systemic Risk

Systemic risk is popularly understood as the risk of collapse of an entire financial system.[1] But systemic risk is also inherent to democracies, because democracies promote centralization and centralization brings fragility. What do I mean by centralization? To visualize this, let's first examine the notion of centralization versus distribution, in an information system:

From Fig. 7.1, it is visible that a central system is "weaker" to a shock than a distributed one. And this is particularly so when the shock affects the centre node (or central nodes, in a decentralized system). But what does this have to do with democracy and investing? Centralization is inherent to democracy, while fractional reserve banking also leads to centralization, because after a wave of bank's defaults (caused by fractional reserve banking), experience shows that democratic regimes install central banks, which enhance centralization!

Under democracy, power lies with the majority, and those in power seek to have absolute power. They must therefore rely on an absolute majority. Hence, every effort is made to create ever greater political structures within a government[2]: Autonomy is stolen from wards or neighbourhoods by municipal governments; municipal governments lose autonomy to provincial or state administrations, and these in turn see their stolen by federal or national governments. The twenty-first century began within a trend of power shift from

---

[1] To some mainstream economists, systemic risk is the risk that the sovereign defaults. This is not our assumption.

[2] Gerrymandering illustrates this point. Gerrymandering is the redrafting of electoral districts, to favour a certain constituency's electoral results.

© The Author(s) 2018
M. Arisson, *Investing in the Age of Democracy*,
https://doi.org/10.1007/978-3-319-95903-0_7

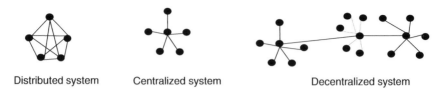

Distributed system   Centralized system   Decentralized system

Fig. 7.1 Centralization and distribution in an information system

nation-states to supranational entities, like the United Nations or the European Union. But at the time of this writing, it has taken a pause (with Brexit).

Financial centralization, on the other hand, was triggered by the acceptance of fractional reserve banking,[3] because this type of banking inevitably creates a credit bubble, its subsequent burst, the bailout or nationalization of the involved banks, and lastly central banks (as illustrated in Fig. 7.2).

On the other hand, as credit expansion and public expenditure are popular, fractional reserve banking was and remains the blood of democracy, because it enables rulers to subsidize today's voters' wishes at the expense of future generations (who do not vote). Any young person seeking to buy his/her first home in the developed world in 2017 understands what I mean here. Hence, central banking and fractional reserve banking make systemic risk (or centralization) possible. We can see this junction between the two already in the early days of the French Revolution, with the issuance of assignats and the Banque of France. Another centralization feature is also associated with fiat currencies, backed by governmental credit. As power shifts to ever bigger governmental structures, so must the support of the fiat currencies. The case of the euro and the support Greece's debt received by the European Central Bank after 2009 is illustrative.

But it is precisely because of this dangerous cocktail that we should not speak of risk, because properly speaking, there is no such a thing. **Whenever fractional reserve banking is present and there is a central bank that enables contagion from banks failures via inflation, the collapse of the financial system is not a risk, but its guaranteed outcome.** In fact, the opposite is true: The tail risk is to actually see economic growth and specialization blossom in an environment of fractional reserve banking, inflation and interest rates intervention.

Until the end of the eighteenth century, systemic risk was limited to the geographic reach of a financial institution. As the ultimate anchor of all banking systems rested in gold, contagion from bank failures, although often

---

[3] According to Dr Huerta de Soto, the Peel Act of July 19, 1844, marks the beginning of this process.

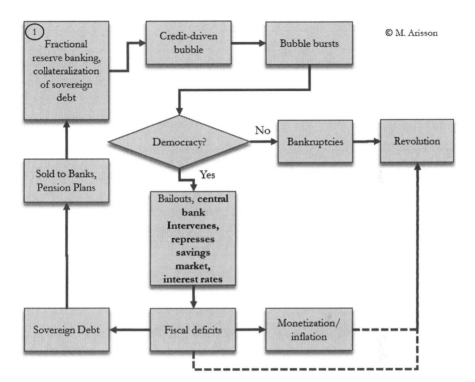

Fig. 7.2 Fractional reserve banking, democracy and intervention

numerous, was fairly limited.[4] With the end of the gold standard system during World War I, and the creation of the gold exchange system, systemic risk took a global dimension.

At this point, a detailed comparison of the different systems we have experienced, so far in the age of democracy, is appropriate. Below, I show the aggregate accounting entries and structures of the main systems in the age of democracy.

---

[4] In Rodgers, Mary Tone and Wilson, Berry K. "Systemic Risk, Missing Gold Flows and the Panic of 1907", The Quarterly Journal of Austrian Economics 14, No. 2 (Summer 2011): 158–187, there is an excellent discussion on the mechanics of adjustments under the gold standard, in reaction to failures. The authors sustain that the gold flows that ensued from Europe into the United States provided the liquidity necessary to mitigate the panic, without the need of intervention. This success in reducing systemic risk was due to the existence of US corporate bonds (mainly from railroads) with coupon and principal payable in gold, in bearer or registered form (at the option of the holder) that facilitated transferability, tradable jointly in the US and European exchanges, and within a payment system operating largely outside of the bank clearinghouse systems. The official story is however that the system was saved by a $25MM JP Morgan-led pool of liquidity injected to the call loan market.

Gold Standard

Under the **gold standard** monetary system, which one can venture[5] to say took place between 1815 and 1914, every central bank issues currency against gold reserves, making exchange rates between currencies mere ratios between the respective gold reserves (Fig. 7.3).

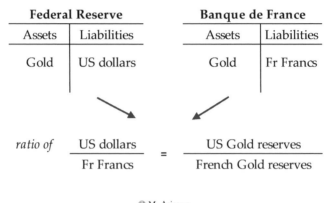

© M. Arisson

Fig. 7.3   Balance sheets of central banks under the gold standard

The gold standard, when left to act without government intervention, is simply a distributed monetary system: A distributed network of gold vaults. As such, it can withstand shocks. However, if a monetary system is under the gold standard and without fractional reserve banking, the nature of these shocks can never be systemic, but limited to those sectors that fall prey to the ever present creative destruction (Fig. 7.4).

Gold Exchange Standard

Under the **gold exchange standard** however (de facto in place from the fall of the KreditAnstalt, in 1931, to 1971), one sovereign holds gold as reserve and its currency is then issued and held as reserve by other central banks. The latter are only indirectly backed by gold. This was the case with the US dollar. The gold exchange standard began in a cooperative way, between the Bank of England and the Federal Reserve during World War I. These two banks, during the 1920s, had the benefit of issuing currency that served as reserve to

---

[5] "Venture" is the operative word here, because the world never saw a pure gold standard take place.

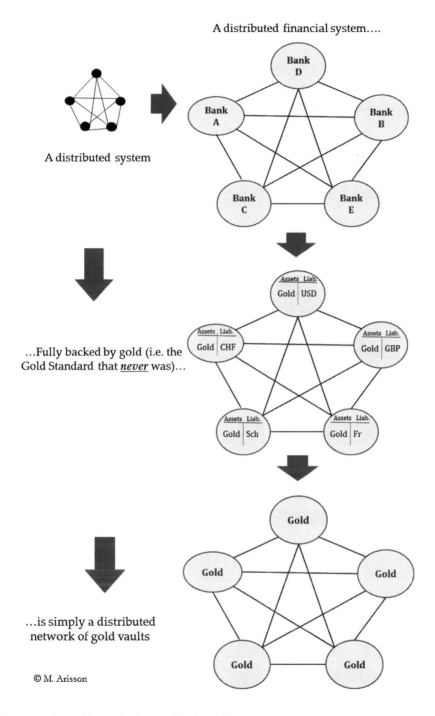

Fig. 7.4 The gold standard, as a distributed system

other central banks. But on May 11, 1931, with the collapse of Austria's KreditAnstalt, a series of bank runs were triggered, in a dramatic test of gold convertibility that would end with a long bank holiday and a gold embargo in the United States in March of 1933, under the administration of F. D. Roosevelt. During this period, in September of 1931, the Bank of England had to break the peg between gold and the sterling pound. From then on and until 1971, the US dollar became the world's reserve currency under a gold exchange standard system that became official in 1944, with the Bretton Woods Conference (Fig. 7.5).

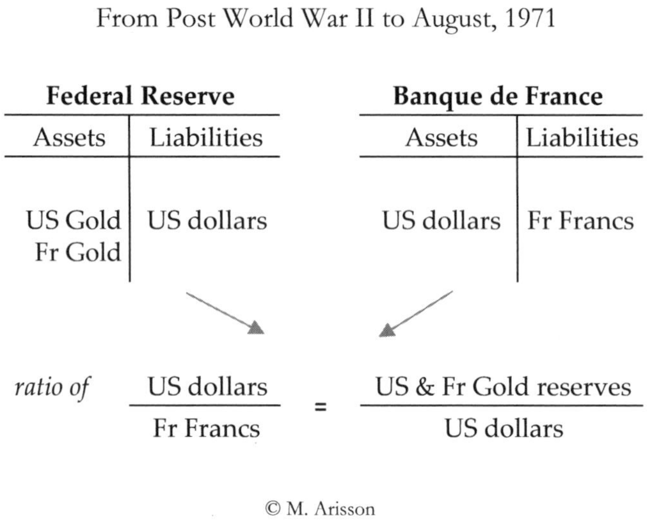

From Post World War II to August, 1971

Federal Reserve		Banque de France	
Assets	Liabilities	Assets	Liabilities
US Gold Fr Gold	US dollars	US dollars	Fr Francs

$$\text{ratio of } \quad \frac{\text{US dollars}}{\text{Fr Francs}} \quad = \quad \frac{\text{US \& Fr Gold reserves}}{\text{US dollars}}$$

© M. Arisson

Fig. 7.5 Balance sheets of central banks under a gold exchange standard, where the US dollar is the reserve currency

Under the gold *exchange* standard, if the sovereign that keeps the privilege of holding the gold also expands its (reserve) currency **secretly** (without a consequent increase in gold), there takes place a wealth transfer, from the holders to the issuer of the reserve currency. Such is the case today, where the Chinese salaried workforce sustains the consumption of the developed world. Structurally speaking thus, the gold *exchange* standard is a centralized system and, as such, was far weaker than its predecessor. It lasted only 40 years, if one takes 1931 as the starting date. This system is a simple time bomb of promised gold redeemability waiting to be tested (Fig. 7.6).

The mechanism through which this wealth transfer occurs was set in earnest during the 1920s, through a contract called currency swap. During the gold exchange standard therefore, either the Federal Reserve or the Bank of England would swap US dollars or pounds with other central banks, in exchange for

A centralized financial system

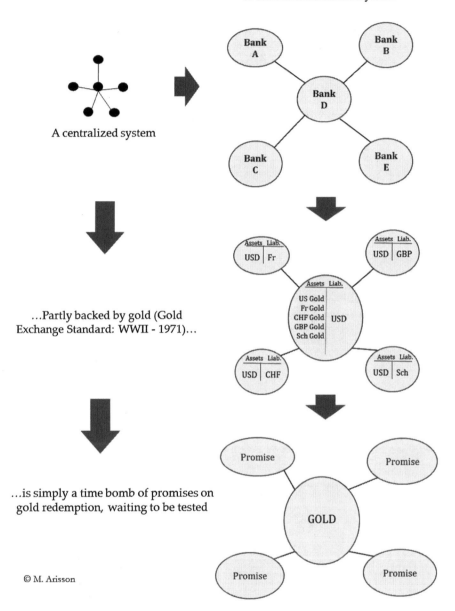

A centralized system

...Partly backed by gold (Gold
Exchange Standard: WWII - 1971)...

...is simply a time bomb of promises on
gold redemption, waiting to be tested

© M. Arisson

Fig. 7.6 The gold exchange standard, as a centralized system

their gold reserves. From Fig. 7.7, which illustrates this mechanism, one can see that the amount of US dollars or sterling pound in circulation increased, without a real counterpart increase in gold. Gold was only swapped from the peripheral central banks' reserves, for US dollars or sterling pound. Although it would seem that only the United States or Great Britain would benefit from this, it was only so in the beginning, because later, additional issuance of their currencies (i.e. USD and £) against a stable quantity of gold would make its way to the peripheral central banks, which in turn could increase their liabilities (i.e. monetary base). The periphery would end up importing inflation.

During the Gold Exchange Standard

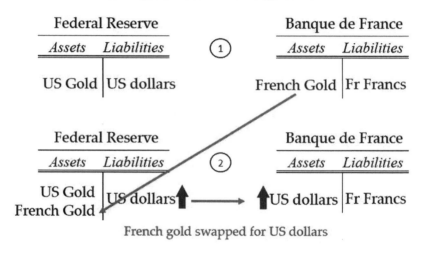

French gold swapped for US dollars

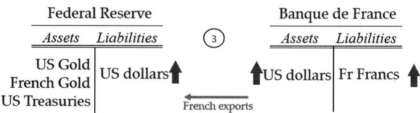

France imports US inflation, exporting goods vs. US dollars
(same as China after Nixon)

Fig. 7.7 Currency swaps during the gold exchange standard

After the gold exchange standard and particularly since 2000, that is, since the creation of the European Monetary Union, we live under a decentralized system. In it, the "nodes" can be represented by the Federal Reserve, the European Central Bank, the Bank of Japan, the People's Bank of China, and probably the Bank of England and the Swiss National Bank. The main nodes however are the first three (Figs. 7.8 and 7.9).

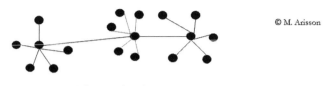

A decentralized system

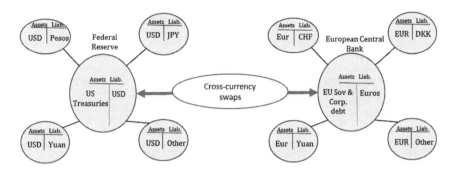

...Full backed by sovereign debt (Since the Fall of the Berliner Wall), with the prominent roles of European Central Bank, (and other CBs) there is a fragile de-centralization

Fig. 7.8 Currency swaps since 2000, in a decentralized system

From 2000 to date

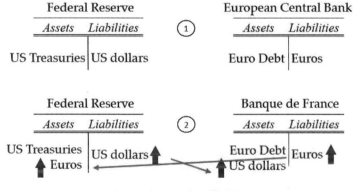

Euros swapped for US dollars

Fig. 7.9 The accounting entries of currency swaps since 2000

Currency swaps between central banks enable systemic risk to gain a global dimension and it is the duty of every investor to fully understand them. To the uneducated, systemic risk is caused by "animal spirits", "herd behaviour" and panics, and the way he seeks to address it is by running correlation scenarios or stress tests. To the educated investor, **there is no systemic risk but mere political decisions** within a process that inevitably ends in contagion and is managed all along with currency swaps.

How It All Began

A currency swap is a contract between two central banks. As such, it cannot precede them. Currency swaps were born in 1922, during an International Monetary Conference that took place in Geneva. The goal of this conference was to stabilize exchange rates (in terms of gold) back to pre-World War I levels. According to Prof. Giovanni B. Pittaluga (Univ. di Genova),[6] there were two key resolutions from the conference, which (in my view) opened the door to currency swaps. Resolution No. 9 proposed that central banks:

[C]entralize and coordinate the demand for gold, and so avoid those wide fluctuations in the purchasing power of gold which might otherwise result from the simultaneous and competitive efforts of a number of countries to secure metallic reserves.

Resolution No. 9 also spelled how the cooperation among central banks would work, which:

[S]hould embody some means of economizing the use of gold maintaining reserves in the form of foreign balance, such, for example, as the gold exchange standard or an international clearing system.

Resolution No. 11 stated that:

The convention will thus be based on a gold exchange standard. (…) A participating country, in addition to any gold reserve held at home, may maintain in any other participating country reserves of approved assets in the form of bank balances, bills, short-term Securities, or other suitable liquid assets … when progress permits, certain of the participating countries will establish a free market in gold and thus become gold centers.

---

[6] See *The Genoa Conference and the Gold Exchange Standard,* con E. Seghezza, Università di Genova, Disefin working paper, n. 7, 2008.

Lastly, gold or foreign exchange would back no less than 40% of the monetary base of central banks (in other words, it allowed for the dilution of the reserves of a currency from 100% to 40%). With this agreement, the stage was set to manage liquidity in a coordinated way and to a degree the world had never witnessed. The reserve multiplier, composed by gold and foreign exchange, could be "managed" through an international clearing system. It could be managed on a global scale.

How Adjustments Worked Under the Gold Standard

Before 1922, adjustments (of financial imbalances) within the gold standard involved the free movement of gold. In Fig. 7.10, we can see how an adjustment would have looked like, as the United States underwent a balance of trade deficit with France,[7] for instance.

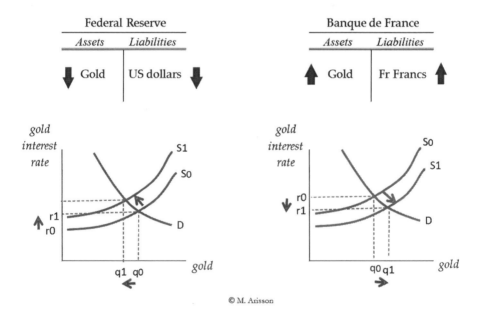

© M. Arisson

Fig. 7.10 Monetary adjustments under the gold standard

---

[7] A balance of trade deficit is the difference between exports from and imports to a nation or a currency zone.

Gold would have left the United States, reducing the asset side of the balance sheet of the Federal Reserve. Matching this movement, the monetary base (i.e. US dollars) would have had to fall too. The gold would have eventually entered the balance sheet of the Banque de France, which would have issued a corresponding marginal amount of French francs, to keep the convertibility rate (of francs to gold). Note that the interest rate, in gold, would have increased in the United States (from r0 to r1), providing a stabilizing mechanism, to repatriate the gold that originally left, thanks to arbitraging opportunities. As Brendan Brown (currently Head of Economic Research at Mitsubishi UFJ Securities International) explained, with free determination of interest rates and even considerable price fluctuations, agents in this system had the legitimate expectation that key relative prices would return to a "perpetual" level. This expectation provided *"…the negative real interest rate which Bernanke so desperately tries to create today with hyped inflation expectations…*[8]*"*

How Adjustments Worked Under the Gold Exchange Standard

During the 1920s and particularly with the stock imbalances resulting from World War I,[9] the search for sustainable financing of reparation payments began. Complicating things, the beginning of this decade saw hyperinflationary processes in Germany and Hungary. In 1924, England and the United States rolled out a plan known as Dawes Plan, and between 1926 and 1928, the Poincaré Stabilization Plan took place in France. As Fig. 7.7 shows, against a stable stock of gold, fiat currency would be loaned between central banks. In the case of a swap for the Banque de France, US dollars would be available/ loaned, which were supposedly backed by gold. The reserve multiplier versus gold expanded, of course. With these transactions, central banks would now be able to influence monetary (i.e. paper) interest rates. The balancing mechanism provided by gold interest rate differentials had been lost. As we saw under the gold standard before, an outflow of US dollars would have caused US dollar rates to rise, impacting the purchasing power of Americans. Now, the reserve multiplier versus gold expanded and the purchasing power of the nation that provided the financing was left untouched (because no gold had to leave the United States, leaving interest rates unchanged). The US dollar would depreci-

---

[8] Brown, Brendan: "The Global Curse of the Federal Reserve: How Its Monetary Virus Stimulates Destructive Waves of Irrational Exuberance and Depression", Murray N. Rothbard Memorial Lecture, presented at the A.E.R. Conference, 21 March 2013, Auburn, AL, ref.: https://www.youtube.com/watc h?v=INDZe4KAZS4&feature=youtu.be&t=19m

[9] By stock imbalances I refer to the enormous debts accumulated by both the Allies (e.g. Great Britain with Argentina) and the Germany.

ate (on the margin and ceteris paribus) against the countries benefiting from these swaps. Inflation was exported from the issuing nation (the United States) to the receiving nations (Europe). The party lasted until 1931 when the collapse of the KreditAnstalt triggered a unanimous wave of deflation.

How the Perspective Changed as the United States Became a Debtor Nation

Fast forward to 1965, two decades after World War II, and currency swaps are no longer seen as a tool to temporarily "stabilize" the financing of flows, like balance of trade deficits or war reparation payments, but stocks of debt. By 1965, central bankers were already concerned with the creation of reserve assets, just like they are today; with the creation of collateral.[10]

On May 31, 1965, the Group of Ten presented what was called the Ossola Report,[11] after Rinaldo Ossola, chairman of the study group involved in its preparation and also vice-chairman of the Bank of Italy. This report specifically addressed the creation of reserve assets. At least back then, gold was still considered to be one of them. In what amounts to a confession (because this document was initially restricted), the Ossola Group declared that the problem:

> [A]rises from the considered expectation that the future flow of gold into reserves cannot be prudently relied upon to meet all needs for an expansion of reserves associated with a growing volume of world trade and payments and that the contribution of dollar holdings to the growth of reserves seems unlikely to continue as in the past.

And here resurfaces an old fallacy: That the quantity of money needs to grow in association with economic growth and particularly that the latter can be conceived in terms of "volume". This fallacy became very popular during the twentieth century and remains so until this day. It is damaging and very wrong, because the efficiency of money actually increases the scarcer it becomes. Scarce money is the secret behind the spectacular, unplanned and spontaneous economic growth witnessed during the nineteenth century in the West. However, currency swaps were once again considered part of the solution. Under the so-called currency assets, the swaps were included by the Ossola Group, as a useful tool for the creation of alternative reserves. Three

---

[10] Refer this excellent post by Zerohedge on the subject: "Desperately Seeking $11.2 Trillion In Collateral, Or How "Modern Money" Really Works", May 1, 2013.

[11] Refer http://www.bis.org/publ/gten_b.pdf

months later, during a Hearing before the Subcommittee on National Security and International Operations, William McChesney Martin, Jr., at that time Chairman of the Board of Governors of the Federal Reserve System, acknowledged a much greater role to currency swaps in maintaining the role of the US dollar as the global reserve currency. In McChesney Martin's words:

> *Under the swap agreements, both the System (i.e. Federal Reserve System) and its partners make drawings only for the purpose of counteracting the effects on exchange markets and reserve positions of temporary or transitional fluctuations in payments flows. About half of the drawings ever made by the System, and most of the drawings made by foreign central banks, have been repaid within three months; nearly 90 per cent of the recent drawings made by the System and 100 per cent of the drawings made by foreign central banks have been repaid within six months. In any event, no drawing is permitted to remain outstanding for more than twelve months. This policy ensures that drawings will be made, either by the System or by a foreign central, bank, only for temporary purposes and not for the purpose of financing a persistent payments deficit. In all swap arrangements both parties are fully protected from the danger of exchange-rate fluctuations. If a foreign central bank draws dollars, its obligation to repay dollars would not be altered if in the meantime its currency were devalued. Moreover, the drawings are exchanges of currencies rather than credits. For instance, if, say, the National Bank of Belgium draws dollars, the System receives the equivalent in Belgian francs; and since the National Bank of Belgium has to make repayment in dollars, the System is at all times protected from any possibility of loss. Obviously, the same protection is given to foreign central banks whenever the System draws a foreign currency.*
>
> *The interest rates for drawings are identical for both parties. Hence, until one party disburses the currency drawn, there is no net interest burden for either party. Amounts drawn and actually disbursed incur an interest cost, needless to say; the interest charge is generally close to the U.S. Treasury bill rate.*[12]

Essentially, with these currency swaps, foreign central banks, which during World War II had shifted their gold to the United States, became middlemen of a product that was a first-degree derivative of the US dollar and a second-degree derivative of gold. On September 24, 1965, someone called this scheme out. In an article published by *Le Monde*, Jacques Rueff,[13] under the hilarious title *Des plans d'irrigation pendant le déluge* (i.e. Irrigation plans during the flood) minced no words and wrote:

---

[12] Statement of William McChesney Martin, Jr., Chairman, Board of Governors of the Federal Reserve System, before the Subcommittee on National Security and International Operations of the Committee on Government Operations United States Senate August 30, 1965. Refer: https://fraser.stlouisfed.org/files/docs/historical/martin/martin65_0830.pdf

[13] Jacques Rueff (1896–1978) was a French economist and adviser to Prime Minister Charles De Gaulle, in 1958.

C'est un euphémisme inacceptable et une scandaleuse hypocrisie que de qualifier de création de "liquidités internationales" les multiples opérations, telles que (currency) swaps…C'est commettre une fraude de même nature que de présenter comme la conséquence d'une insuffisance générale de liquidités l'insuffisance des moyens dont disposent les États-Unis et l'Angleterre pour le règlement de leur déficit extérieur.

My translation: "…It is an unacceptable euphemism and an outrageous hypocrisy to qualify as creation of" international liquidity "multiple transactions, like (currency) swaps" "…In the same fashion, it is a fraud to present as the consequence of a general lack of liquidity, the lack of means available to the USA and England to settle their external deficits….[14]"

Comparing the United States and England to underdeveloped countries, Rueff added that these also lack external resources, but those that are needed cannot be provided to them but by credit operations rather than by monetary invention disguised as necessary and in the general interest of the public (i.e. rest of the world). With impressive prediction, Rueff warned that the problem would present itself in all its greatness, the day the United States and England decide to recover their financial independence by reimbursing with their dangerous liabilities (i.e. currencies). That day, said Rueff, international coordination would be necessary and legitimate. But such coordination would not revolve around the creation of alternative instruments of reserve, demanded by a starving-for-liquidity world. That day would be a day of liquidation, where debtors and creditors would be equally interested and would share the common responsibility of the lightness with which they jointly accepted the monetary difficulties that are present. Sadly, Rueff's call still sounds familiar in the twenty-first century.

How Adjustments Work Without Currency Swaps

Until the end of the gold exchange standard, even if the reserve multiplier suppressed the value of gold (as it does today), gold was still the ultimate reserve and had no counterparty risk. After August 15, 1971, the day when Nixon issued the Executive Order 11615, the ultimate reserve has been simply cash (i.e. US dollars) or its counterparty, US Treasuries. And unlike gold, these reserve assets can be created or destroyed ex nihilo. When they are rehypothecated, leverage grows unlimited and when their value falls, valuations

---

[14] Here one must consider the reverse mechanism: Without currency swaps, the United States would not have the trade deficits they have. To put this in context, if President Trump was serious about addressing trade deficits without affecting free trade, his administration would have to intervene the Federal Reserve and forbid currency swaps with other central banks.

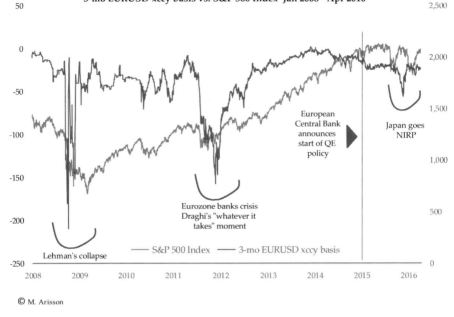

Fig. 7.11 EURUSD cross-currency basis as an indicator of liquidity stress (a.k.a. systemic risk)

dive unstoppably. **Because (and unlike in 1907) the transmission channel for these reserves today is the banking system, when they become scarce, counterparty risk inevitably morphs into systemic risk.**

When Rueff discussed currency swaps, he had imbalances in mind. In the twenty-first century, we no longer have the luxury of worrying about them. Balance of trade deficits? Current account deficits? Fiscal deficits? In the twenty-first century, the only thing we have in mind is counterparty risk within the financial system, or systemic risk. The thermometer that measures this risk used to be the Eurodollar swap basis (Fig. 7.11) until European Central Bank's President Mario Draghi further removed the link between the euro and the US dollar, when Quantitative Easing began in earnest in 2015.

When the US dollar is the carry currency, the cost of accessing it is the global benchmark for what market practitioners call "risk". When, for instance, they say "risk sold off", what they mean is that the cost of the carry currency increased.

In Fig. 7.11, we can see two big gaps in the Eurodollar swap basis.[15] The one in 2008 corresponds to the Lehman event. The other one, in 2011, corresponds to the banking crisis in the Eurozone that was contained with a

---

[15] The Eurodollar swap basis is a bilateral contract where a sum borrowed in euros is converted into US dollars. At expiration, the principal is converted back from US dollars to euros at the agreed (upfront) fixed currency rate.

reduction in the cost of USDEUR swaps and with the Long-Term Refinancing Operations done by the European Central Bank. In both events, the financial system was in danger and banks were forced to delever. How would the adjustment process have worked, had there not been currency swaps to extend?

In Fig. 7.12, I explain the adjustment process, in the **absence of** a currency swap. As we see in step one, the assumption is a spike in the sovereign default risk of the Eurozone, which affects banks. Given the default risk of sovereign debt held by Eurozone banks, capital leaves the Eurozone, appreciating the US dollar. We see loan loss reserves increase (bringing the aggregate value of assets and equity down). As these banks have liabilities in US dollars and take deposits in euros, this mismatch and the devaluation of the euro deteriorates their risk profile. Eurozone banks are forced to liquidate their US dollar loan portfolios,

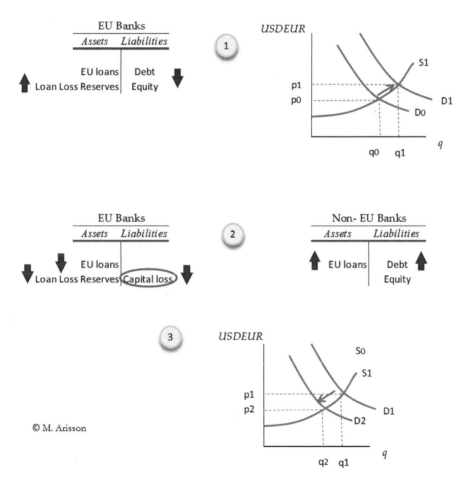

Fig. 7.12 An adjustment under fiat currency standard, without currency swaps

shown in step two. As they sell them below par, the banks have to book losses. The non-Eurozone banks that purchase these loans cannot book immediate gains. We live in a fiat currency world, and banks simply let their loans amortize; there's no mark to market. With these purchases, capital re-enters the Eurozone, depreciating the US dollar versus the euro. In the end, there is no credit crunch. As long as this process is left to the market to work itself out smoothly, borrowers don't suffer, because ownership of the loans is simply transferred.

This is neutral to sovereign risk, but going forward, if the sovereigns don't improve their risk profile, lending capacity will be constrained. In the end, an adjustment takes place in (a) the foreign exchange market, (b) the value of the bank capital of Eurozone banks, and (c) the amount of capital being transferred from outside the Eurozone into the Eurozone.

How Adjustments Work Today, with Currency Swaps

Let's now proceed to examine the adjustment—or, better said, lack thereof—in the presence of currency swaps. The adjustment is delayed. In the figure below, we can see that the Fed intervenes indirectly, lending to Eurozone banks through the European Central Bank. Capital does not leave the United States. Dollars are printed instead and the US dollar depreciates. On November 30, 2011, upon the Fed's announcement at 8 a.m. of a new EURUSD currency swap, the euro gained two cents versus the US dollar. As no capital is transferred, no further savings are required to sustain the Eurozone and the misallocation of resources can continue, because no loans are sold. This was bullish of (Eurozone) sovereign risk. The Fed became a creditor of the Eurozone. If systemic risk had deteriorated in the Eurozone, the Fed would have been forced to first keep reducing the cost of the swaps and later to roll them indefinitely, as long as there remained at least a European Central Bank as a counterparty for the Fed,[16] to avoid an increase in interest rates in the US dollar funding market. But if the Eurozone broke up, there would not be any "safe" counterparty—at least in the short term—for the Fed to lend US dollars to. In the presence of a European central bank, the swaps would be bullish for gold. In the absence of one, the difficulty in establishing swap lines would temporarily be very bearish for gold (and the rest of the assets) (Fig. 7.13).

---

[16] This observation is not idle. Should the sustainability of the Eurozone be put in doubt (as with important country members leaving the zone), the efficiency of currency swaps would be seriously impaired, precisely at a time of heightened capital movements.

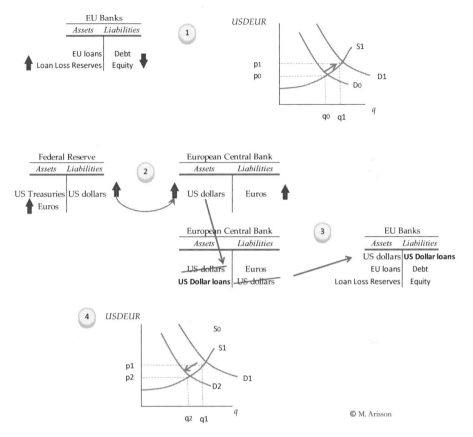

Fig. 7.13 An adjustment under fiat currency standard, with currency swaps

For over a century, we witnessed the slow and progressive destruction of the best global mechanism available to cooperate in the creation and allocation of resources. This destruction began with the loss of the ability to address flow imbalances (i.e. savings, trade). After the world wars, we also lost the ability to address stock imbalances, and by 1971 we ensured that any price flexibility left to reset the system in the face of an adjustment would be wiped out too. This occurred in two steps: First at a global level, with the irredeemability of gold (the world would no longer be able to repudiate the imposition of credit as money) and, second, at an intertemporal level, with zero interest rates: At an aggregate level, countries can no longer produce consumption adjustments. From 2015, adjustments can only make way through a growing series of global systemic risk events with increasingly relevant consequences. Currency swaps have always been ignored and hidden, to say the least. On January 29, 2016, in the face of a massive capital outflow, China needed a currency swap with the Fed, to protect whatever was left of USD reserves.[17] However, to save face, a currency swap was only mildly announced and indirectly set up, with the Bank of Japan. In the future, as central banks lose control (refer next lesson) I believe that swaps, as a tool, will no longer be able to face the upcoming challenges. When this fact sets in, governments will be forced to resort directly to basic confiscation (of assets used for debt settlement). The latest developments in central banking in 2016 suggest this view may be correct if cash is outlawed in support of negative interest rates.

Conclusion: There Are No Black Swans

Investors today continue to believe in two wrong ideas. The first one is the belief in the existence of something called systemic risk and that said risk can be monitored or understood with the use of statistical methods. The collapse of the entire financial system is not a risk but the natural and logical outcome resulting from precise, explicit and purposeful actions carried out by monetary authorities.

The second belief is that this risk can be understood as a tail risk and is commonly called a "black swan". If this were so, we would have to know the entire risk distribution and be able to observe, over time, a convergence towards a defined value. But this, as we know from our discussions on decidability, is not possible. It is easy to assume that because statistical analysis will always lag events, all of a sudden and under shock, one can speak of "tail" risk, of a phenomenon outside parameters previously considered. But that would be intellectually dishonest, especially when we already know the causes (i.e. the historical development of centralization and swaps discussed in the paragraphs above).

In light of this, what can we do to protect ourselves? I am inclined however to resort to a trading (not investing) strategy: To use options. But currency swaps are over-the-counter instruments and there is no options market for them. It is a pity, because for banks, correlation trades or hedging of credit default risk may not be efficient (because the bank may not get capital relief from the hedge). Nor is it to follow Basel III "recommendations" to enhance capital and liquidity. Their Treasury Groups should be able to continuously be long out-of-the-money calls on EURUSD, JPYUSD, CNYUSD or other crosses basis, on a rolling basis. This is the hedge that goes to the core of the problem, not their indirect consequences (i.e. credit default waves, capital shortages, etc.).

---

[17] Nobody really knows what the People's Bank of China holds as reserves, and how much.

Bibliography

Rodgers, Mary Tone and Wilson, Berry K.. (Summer 2011). Systemic Risk, Missing Gold Flows and the Panic of 1907. *The Quarterly Journal of Austrian Economics* Vol 14, No. 2. Pp. 158–187.

Seghezza, E. (2008). *The Genoa Conference and the Gold Exchange standard.* Università di Genova, Disefin working paper, n. 7.

Brown, Brendan. (March 2013). *The Global Curse of the Federal Reserve: How Its Monetary Virus Stimulates Destructive Waves of Irrational Exuberance and Depression.* Murray N. Rothbard Memorial Lecture, presented at the Austrian Economics Research Conference, Auburn, AL. Retrieved March 2013 from: https://www.youtube.com/watch?v=INDZe4KAZS4&feature=youtu.be&t=19m

Anonymous. (May 1, 2013). *Desperately Seeking $11.2 Trillion In Collateral, Or How "Modern Money" Really Works.* Retrieved from https://www.zerohedge.com/news/2013-05-01/desperately-seeking-112-trillion-collateral-or-how-modern-money-really-works

Group of Ten. (May 31, 1965). *Report of the study group on the creation of reserve assets.* Report to the Deputies of The Group of Ten. Retrieved April 2013 from http://www.bis.org/publ/gten_b.pdf

Rueff, Jacques. (1971). *Le péché monétaire de l'Occident.* Chapitre XI, p. 177. Paris: CD Librairie Plon.

Statement of William McChesney Martin, Jr., Chairman, Board of Governors of the Federal Reserve System, before the Subcommittee on National Security and International Operations of the Committee on Government Operations United States Senate Aug. 30, 1965. Retrieved May 2013 from https://fraser.stlouisfed.org/files/docs/historical/martin/martin65_0830.pdf

8

Inflation and Hyperinflation

The Concept of Inflation

Inflation, in increasing degrees, has been present since the time of the American and French revolutions. Indeed, inflation had already taken place in ancient times, and Spain experienced it in the sixteenth century, but these historical events pale in comparison with the inflationary episodes of modern times.

During the French Revolution, the lands of the Church mostly, and of some noblemen, were confiscated to back legal tender notes issued by the revolutionary authorities. The notes were called *assignats*[1] and were backed by real estate. It didn't take long to see the number of printed assignats escalate exponentially, backed by a fixed amount of land, although I doubt anyone ever held any hope of redeeming these notes. Thus, at end of the eighteenth century, without a central bank (as we know it today), the most powerful nation in the European continent was able to create a veritable hyperinflation. In 1794 the Louis d'Or (French gold coin issued since 1640, approx. 6.75 grams) was worth 75 livres papier. By April 1795, it had reached 200 livres papier. In May 1795, it had reached 325 livres, and by October, 2000 livres.[2]

An eternal characteristic of inflationary processes is scarcity or a violent drop of production. This is exactly the opposite of what we, in the twentieth and twenty-first centuries, have been and continue to be taught: That inflation is a policy tool to reach full employment and increase production. Yet, reality shows the opposite, time after time. The most recent examples are

---

[1] Pierre Gaxotte, *La Révolution Française,* Paris, Éditions Tallandier, 2014.
[2] Idem.

© The Author(s) 2018
M. Arisson, *Investing in the Age of Democracy,*
https://doi.org/10.1007/978-3-319-95903-0_8

Zimbabwe, Venezuela or Argentina. Across geographies, cultures or ages, the results are always the same: Inflation destroys production and productivity, leaving higher unemployment and misery. And it makes sense: With the destruction of money, an institution so vital for enabling social coordination, specialization and productivity vanish.

What is inflation? Inflation is popularly understood today as a general increase in prices. By general, I mean more or less unanimous. By prices, it is meant prices of final consumer goods. There are those who believe this increase is caused by "structural" forces, like scarcity of raw materials or mystical "rigidities" of "production functions". Others, better informed, understand that it is the result of what is also commonly known as "money printing". Fewer still know how "money printing" takes place. It is not my intention to write about economics here, but given the relevance of inflation to investment performance, I must devote a few lines to examine it and its connection to democratic regimes.

Inflation is the creation of legal tender (not necessarily for all debts or market participants, but even for some debts or market participants) by coercive means. This definition implies the necessary involvement of an authority imposing the newly created tendering instrument and the helplessness of those affected by the imposition. What people commonly refer to as "inflation" is the creation of government's fiat currency. In any case, any inflationary event (i.e. any creation of any legal tender) can, by definition, never be neutral: It always affects relative prices. Those who have the privilege of being the first to use the new legal tender will always use it to purchase goods at prices *before* its creation (i.e. old prices). In so doing, they affect those prices only, initiating a series of concatenated changes in relative prices, which affect economic calculation. **Inflation is never neutral, and it is precisely because it is never neutral that it exists!** If it was neutral, rulers would have no incentive to create it. If I can save $20,000 per year and a car costs $20,000, I will make the same decision in relation to it if my savings capacity and the price of the car both suddenly spike to $40,000.

What has confused the world over in the twenty-first century is the idea that inflation is only caused by the creation of money. Inflation encompasses a wider spectrum: As long as a government enforces the creation of any means of payment (i.e. legal tender), there is inflation. In 2008, the legal tender created by the Fed was the funding provided against junk mortgage-backed securities through specific repo facilities. Because these mortgage-backed securities could suddenly be morphed into legal tender within the financial system, we witnessed the impressive recovery in real estate prices and financial stocks in the United States. Since May of 2010, the European Central Bank has intervened progressively. First, it accepted sovereign and supra-sovereign debt as collateral for lending. In January of 2015, it began purchasing sovereign debt outright, in billions per month, at origination. The policy of the European Central Bank made the euro a funding currency, triggering the refinancing of USD corporate debt (i.e. Yankee bonds) for EUR debt. Since then, we witness counterintuitive spikes in the value of the EURUSD every time bad news come out of the Eurozone, because margin calls force the sale of euro-denominated assets and demand of euros to repay debt. When governments allow the cancellation of debt denominated in gold with gold futures contracts, they create inflation in gold and gold is devalued. Thus, to the economically uneducated observer, since 2008 there has been something miscalled "asset inflation", which denotes the idea that it may only be transitory or harmless, because the price of groceries or fuel has not increased. Or even worse, because the prices of assets have not fallen.

In the age of democracy, it is imperative to possess an excellent understanding of the balance sheet of the central bank affecting our investments. In 2016, this means being up to date on what the central banks of the United States, the European Union, China, Japan, the United Kingdom and Switzerland do. Every week, we need to have read and understood their balance sheets and their interventions. All markets are affected by the policies of central banks. For those of us investing capital in a business, the question is this: If as a consequence of the central bank's interventions, the operating costs for this business increase, will the business be able to adapt? Will it be able to raise the price of its products?

There is also a much-neglected angle about the impact on inflation, and it has to do with collections. If there is an ironic feature in the inflationary process, it is that *at hyperinflationary levels* the higher the amount of legal tender issued, the more illiquid the market that is impacted by it becomes. When fiat currency is printed, the market for fiat currency becomes illiquid. This happens because credit (i.e. leverage) disappears and debtors seek to delay payments (to dilute their liabilities). The more illiquid markets become, the harder it is to collect accounts receivable for a firm and the larger its working capital needs grow, precisely at a time when loan interest rates soar. It is a dangerous spiralling process that, if unresolved when hyperinflation kicks in, leads to bankruptcy. Lately, because Basel III regulations have encouraged arbitraging between fractional reserve banking of collateral assets (i.e. US Treasuries) vis-à-vis fiat currency, the US Treasury market has become more illiquid. This latter phenomenon is also known as "repo specialness".

Hyperinflation or How Central Banks Lose Control

As a student, I remember that when inflation and hyperinflation were discussed, every presenter or professor would state that the difference between the two was only one of degree. The argument went like this: "When inflation reaches two digits but is below 100%, one speaks of high inflation. When it surpasses 100% per annum, one is at the gates of hyperinflation." This simplistic view also led to the belief that hyperinflation was rather caused by the mismanagement of expectations of market participants and almost always suggests that indexing of contracts and price controls are available tools to deal with the problem.

One of the concepts that I want to leave to you with absolute clarity is this: **Hyperinflation is not a quantitative characteristic of inflation. It is qualitative**. Hyperinflation does not take place when an arbitrary inflation rate is reached. **Hyperinflation is simply the loss of control by a central bank.** When a central bank loses control, hyperinflation sets in. Now, let me explain what I mean by "loss of control".

Central banks hold assets that back their liabilities. The most important liability is the fiat currency issued, that is imposed to us as legal tender. Fiat currency does not pay interest. Therefore, in a simplified balance sheet, if the assets backing the fiat currency do pay an interest (i.e. government bonds), the central bank should earn income (do not confuse income with profit).

That income, however, could be more than wiped out by a loss in the market value of the assets supporting the currency. The European Central Bank and more recently (i.e. 2015) the Swiss National Bank have experienced such losses. Nevertheless, a one-time loss that would take the central bank's equity to even negative levels does not represent a loss of control by said central bank. It simply doesn't, because as long as the legal tender is not redeemable and its quantity does not spiral out of control, citizens holding it cannot challenge the net worth of the central bank.

A central bank loses control when it is forced to issue an interest-paying liability and suffers a **recurring** net interest loss. This means that the interest it receives from its assets is less than the one it pays on its liabilities:

$$\text{Int. Rate}\,(a) \times \text{Assets} < \text{Int.Rate}\,(l) \times \text{Liabilities}$$

When the above scenario occurs, the central bank has no alternative but to issue more fiat currency to pay for the interest loss. **This loss is called a quasi-fiscal deficit**, and in the absence of any changes, it grows exponentially with the passage of time. In other words, the central bank is forced to monetize the interest loss that it was forced to take, because it was forced to issue high interest-paying liabilities. This is a circularity that can only be resolved with the collapse of the currency: The more it monetizes its losses, the higher the depreciation of the currency, the higher the interest it has to pay on its liabilities, the more it has to monetize its losses.

There are therefore three key conditions that need to be present: (a) The obligation by the central bank to assume interest-paying liabilities, (b) the obligation by the central bank to pay an interest rate on said liabilities higher than the one it earns on its assets (mostly government debt), and (c) the full knowledge of this situation by market participants.

In 2016, a good example was the central bank of Argentina (BCRA or Banco Central de la República Argentina). When Mauricio Macri assumed the presidency of the country in December 2015, the BCRA was bankrupt. The former authorities had managed to keep the value of the peso relatively stable against the US dollar, by selling USD futures at below market prices, which could be used to settle spot transactions in Argentina's financial system (the former president of the BCRA and president of the country are currently facing legal action because of this). Macri thus had a unique opportunity to close the BCRA and establish a free, private money system in the country, at basically no **marginal** cost.[3] He chose however to recapitalize the bank with debt and settle the foreign exchange losses.[4] In so doing, the intention was to be able to access the international USD markets, to supply Argentina (at the provincial and federal levels) with US dollars, while he unfolded a plan of deficit reductions, to gradually eliminate inflation. It is by all means a courageous bet. But let's examine the yield curve of the BCRA (Fig. 8.1).

The yield curve above is that of the BCRA's liabilities. For the week of April 11 to 15, this is what the BCRA reported:

On April 12th, the Banco Central de la República Argentina carried out a Dutch auction of LEBACs in pesos and USD.

For pesos, bids reached $67,347 million, which were all accepted. This implies a partial refinancing of outstandings for $69,182 million, a decrease in circulating stock of $1,938 million and an expansion of the monetary base by $4,583 million. The average maturity of our portfolio fell to 43 days.[5]

---

[3] As the BCRA delayed the fx adjustments, the bank was technically bankrupt. For all relevant purposes, the bank was simply a printing press and one could have easily argued that it was not even trusted as lender of last resort.

[4] President Macri's administration also settled Argentina's fiscal bankruptcy with the respective holdout investors.

[5] Banco Central de la República Argentina, Informe Semanal de Subastas de Lebacs and Nobacs, Week of April 11– 15, 2016 (author's translation).

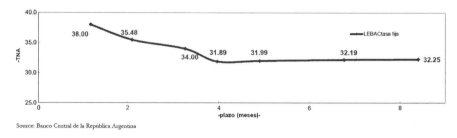

Source: Banco Central de la República Argentina

Fig. 8.1 Banco Central de la República Argentina: yield curve on April 14, 2016

Thus, the BCRA monetized losses for $4583 million pesos. This means that, if the average maturity of the portfolio is 43 days, by July 2016, the BCRA will have to either increase the Lebacs (Letras del Banco Central) rate from 38% if they want to control the inflation rate or allow inflation to spike. My guess is that there will be a mixture of the two, generating further losses, potentially leading the country into a hyperinflationary spiral.

In the age of inflation, or in the age of the democracy, we need to be very vigilant and foresee which monetary policies may eventually corner a central bank into losing control. If accurately predicted, we will be in an enviable position, because it is under these conditions when one can make the trade (not investment) of a lifetime.

In general, loss of control is forced by the collapse of counterparty risk of a systemically important market participant. In its most direct and pure form, it can be the collapse of counterparty risk in the banking system itself. In this regard, it is likely that the recent global trend towards negative interest rates will completely wipe out the profitability of banks (it has already affected significantly their corporate lending operations), forcing central banks to pay interest that will ultimately be needed to maintain the confidence of depositors in the financial system. But loss of control can also be triggered indirectly, by the collapse of counterparty risk in markets that end up engaging the financial system. Examples of these are money markets or the gold market. Should defaults occur in these, the ramifications could be substantial to the point that a central bank must step in and refinance liabilities issuing interest-paying debt, causing a domino effect.

It is worth noting that hyperinflation is more likely to occur in genuine democratic nations, where the power of those in command rests upon the popular vote. This is so because in the face of the collapse of counterparty risk, for reputational reasons, the affected government cannot be seen refinancing banking losses with its own debt. Taxpayers will not tolerate the news that Treasury bills, which will contribute to increase the fiscal deficit, have been issued to rescue a single market participant or a particular market. Democratic governments, eventually, are thus forced to inject the worse remedy (i.e. inflation), because the eventual collapse of the currency destroys the savings of generations, relative prices and productivity, and more often than not is accompanied by loss of lives and property. Any of these scenarios is always accompanied by repression and coercion from the engaged governments, who desperately seek to retain control of the situation. Deposits may be frozen (i.e. Argentina in 2001, Cyprus in 2013), capital movements restricted (i.e. Brazil, Chile or Iceland during the 2008 crisis), contracts indexed (i.e. Berlin's property rentals in 2015) to inflation (at official, not realistic rates), assets taxed (i.e. Vancouver 2016, Toronto 2017) or seized (i.e. the United States in 1933).

These actions destroy production, generate scarcity of goods, trigger black markets and their associated criminality and corruption, and accelerate the collapse of a government and its currency. Depending on the institutional health of the affected government, the transfers of wealth caused by these scenarios will either benefit friends of government (worst case) or those citizens who can foresee them or are lucky (i.e. owners of real estate in Canada at 2003). Experience shows that these scenarios are accompanied by social upheaval and your ultimate personal, subjective assessment of the situation will affect your decision of whether to protect your wealth purchasing movable real assets (worst case) or immovable ones (i.e. real estate).

Addendum

The comments above on the situation in Argentina were written in April, 2016, for the first, self-published edition of this book.

They proved to be incredibly on spot: In April 2018 (i.e. two years later, as suggested in Lesson 1, "Sovereign Risk, Fallacy No. 3: Sovereign debt in local currency cannot default"), Argentina's central bank could almost not refinance its short-term debt (i.e. Lebacs). Between April 16, 2018, and May 15, 2018, the peso devalued from 20 to 25 versus the US dollar, proving my point: To believe that a government cannot default on its debt, if the same is denominated in its own currency, is a fallacy.

Buyers of Lebacs lost 25% of principal (in US dollars), Argentina's banks were forced to sell US dollar holdings (they were deliberately pushed to insolvency as their market capitalization plunged), and the government had to request a stand-by arrangement from the International Monetary Fund.

This also proves that having lost control of the situation (the central bank had to accept paying a minimum 40% interest rate on their short-term peso liabilities), Argentina in June 2018 is seriously headed towards a hyperinflationary scenario.

Bibliography

Banco Central de la República Argentina, Informe Semanal de Subastas de Lebacs and Nobacs, April 11– 15, 2016.

Rodríguez, Carlos Alfredo. (Septiembre 1993). Economic Consequences of Quasi-Fiscal Deficits. *CEMA Working Papers*. No. 91. Retrieved May 2014 from https://www.ucema.edu.ar/publicaciones/download/documentos/91.pdf.

9

Real Capital Assets

It is generally believed that one's savings can be safe if they are invested in real assets. This is not always true and if it is, it is not fully true either in democratic regimes. In the following sections, I identify a few typical real capital assets, which are common investment targets, and briefly discuss them.

Movable Real Assets

Cattle

Of all the real capital assets available, cattle is probably the most expensive one. Cattle is a capital asset because it can produce a stable income in the form of offspring. But cattle requires maintenance. The investor can rent land for it, but the land will still need to provide good pastures and fencing. Alternatively, a feedlot can be operated, in which case, the supply of food for the cattle will have to be outsourced. Cattle requires labour, veterinary expenses and its price can be very volatile. Owning it will probably demand a vanilla hedging strategy too.

For the investor, the advantage of owning cattle is that there is no fixed recipe for managing it, and it is open to so many improvements, where productivity can be enhanced and profits increased. Cattle is a movable real capital asset and, as such, is also subject to the vagaries of location. For instance, if I own cattle and find out that the demographics of a particular location is suddenly growing exponentially, I can anticipate a growing demand for meat there. An example is the discovery of a mine, or oil or gas shale, which will

© The Author(s) 2018
M. Arisson, *Investing in the Age of Democracy*,
https://doi.org/10.1007/978-3-319-95903-0_9

demand the establishment of a significant workforce. Those in the cattle business can move the cattle as near there as possible to establish a dominant market position.

In terms of operations, little improvements in diet can also yield better returns on the capital. And a good marketing plan can also position this real capital asset in a better place. Above all, what I like in cattle is the fact that one has room to manoeuvre with the investment, and that at least in physical terms (i.e. number of calves per mother), income can be predicted with relative accuracy.

Wine

Wine is also a movable capital asset. Unlike cattle and trees, wine does not offer an income. It is a zero-coupon investment, albeit with negative carry.[1] This means that only at maturity (whenever that is), one recovers the value of principal, accrued by the mere passage of time. The negative carry consists of the storage costs associated with the investment, including insurance.

From the above definition, one can also make the case that a bottle purchased from a chateau to store is not a capital asset, but work in progress. The storing part, which takes years, is the final stage of the production process.[2] There are however specific characteristics that make this capital asset a risky bet. To start, wine is not homogeneous. Not even from the same chateau, as the market discriminates among vintages. This can play against or in favour of the seller. But there is also the issue of determining when to sell. Although wine can be thought of as a zero-coupon investment, its maturity is nowhere determined ex ante.

Wine can be sold privately (i.e. over the counter), but there are three wine exchanges in the United Kingdom: The London International Vintners Exchange (Liv-ex), the Berry Bros. & Rudd (BBC) and the Cavex. The Liv-ex has additional sub-indices. As an asset class, it has been studied in comparison to others,[3] indiscriminately using the tools that I object at the beginning of this book. To apply statistical analysis to a product that is not homogeneous makes no sense to me. Wine is differentiated along pedigree, longevity, marketability and critics. For this reason, perhaps the most relevant factor to succeed with this asset is our marketing skills.

---

[1] This means that there is a net cash outflow necessary to "carry" this asset in inventory.
[2] I am not aware of the tax considerations associated with this perspective.
[3] Ref. Philippe Masset and Jean-Philippe Weisskopf's Working Paper 57, from the American Association of Wine Economists, March 2010.

Unmovable Real Assets

Forests

Like wine, forests are also a zero-coupon investment *in real estate*, with negative carry. But we have more latitude: the maturity of this investment is an interval; it has a minimum holding period, but investors can speculate as to when to sell the produce. Once sold, if not replanted, we are still left with the principal: The land.

It would seem that the investment is in the land and forestry is a business, therefore, not quite qualifying for our definition of a capital asset. But the defining point is that the planted trees grow with time, regardless of what we do, as long as we pay the maintenance costs (i.e. the negative carry). The lumber can also be stored for a long period, to demand a better price, or its price hedged in the futures market.

What I find attractive in forestry is that the fundamentals of probability theory can clearly be applied. We no longer deal with unique historical events to extrapolate arbitrarily and forecast returns, as modern finance would like us to do. We can scientifically estimate physical returns on timberland, given weather, soil and other conditions. And we can also establish a floor, hedging the final price.

In addition, because we deal with trees (who do not vote), democratic regimes do not have a view on yield caps for timberland (as they do with rental income, to protect tenants, who do vote and are more numerous than landlords). The only concern is environmental sustainability. Therefore, forestry constitutes a relatively safe and simple way to manage an investment, as long as we find the right cost structure, including the price of the land.

Residential Real Estate

Let me begin by clarifying that the house or apartment you live in falls outside this analysis: it is not an investment. Having said it, at this late stage in the age of democracy, where building regulations, legislation biased against landlords and capping profits are the norm (some examples in 2016 are Berlin, Vancouver, London and soon …Toronto), it is probably not too far-fetched to imagine that residential property is no longer an income-producing investment. From a practical point, one must also add property management fees to the profitability equation, because in this global world, it is reasonable to expect that real estate investors will not be geographically close to their properties and, therefore, they need to outsource their management.

Compared to public markets, there is one feature I like from real estate, which is also pivotal in defining its value: Location. Location is a unique characteristic of each property and it means that, unlike so many other securities, a property title on residential property cannot fall prey to a Ponzi scheme. There cannot be multiple property titles over a residence, and therefore, its value cannot be manipulated. In this respect, real estate is like an investment in art: Unique. But because it is not movable, it can and has been subject to significant taxation. Prof. Miguel A. Bastos with reason notes that, in fact, we have no property rights over real estate, but only usufruct. This means that we can only enjoy its use. It is not unusual to see in a developed country, for instance, a landlord pay on average 0.8% to 1% per year in property tax over the assessed value of his property (i.e. assessed by the same government!). He has de facto no control over the value assessed by the taxing authority (i.e. municipality), and if he refuses payment, eventually the property is seized from him and he can no longer enjoy its use. The property tax is evidently used to fund infrastructure, but its payment is coercive and there is no guarantee that said infrastructure will directly affect, in a positive way, either the landlord or the property, which is subject to expropriation at any time, on the grounds of "public interest". Should the landlord oppose the seizure, he will end up in prison. Should he seek to escape from prison, he will be shot down by police. Therefore, he is not really a landlord, but a usufructuary. The purchase price of real estate, in this case, represents an upfront payment on the transferable right to enjoy it. But only the government owns it.

Real estate is usually sought after as a safe investment, particularly in times of inflation. But when I look to countries with a history of high inflation, I fail to see safety in real estate. Inflation destroys savings and makes the poor poorer. At the same time, there is always a phase in which interest rates spike (when hyperinflation takes off) that drives property values down. At such times, tenants lose their jobs, those who had purchased real estate with debt see their investments foreclosed and governments put caps on rents and raise property taxes to cover deficits. All these factors end up defeating the purpose of buying real estate in the first place: If the situation is too bad, tenants can even end up claiming possession of the property. There is also another dynamic to keep in mind. When inflation is relevant, the local currency depreciates, and at some point, real estate trades in foreign currency (i.e. US dollars in Latin America). But it is very common to see foreign exchange controls imposed at such times, making any possibility of selling the property and collecting the proceeds just a dream. The real estate market freezes as owners decide not to sell and wait for the storm to pass.

But if the comments above were correct, how is it that we see a significant investment activity in residential properties even in 2016 in places like Canada, for instance? The driver behind these investments is not the search for income but for gain and, somehow, safety too. In this respect, real estate is no longer an investment but a trade with negative carry. It is obvious that the trade is fully fuelled by monetary policy, but its analysis falls beyond the scope of this book.

Farmland

It is generally believed that farmland is a good place to park one's wealth in times of financial repression. There is some truth to that, but history shows that this is only so as long as the financial repression is limited. Farmers, land-owners will always be loathed by democracies, because, in many ways, they can afford to ignore democratic rulers and carry on with a self-sufficient living. This is particularly so the more a government represses money, making farmers their preferred scapegoats. It was so in Ancient Egypt, during the fall of the Roman Empire, in France during the Revolution, or in Argentina and Zimbabwe in the twentieth century, and Venezuela in the twenty-first century. Farmers are thus the first to protest authority and their economic independence represents a cause for concern to the democratic ruler.

Often, during the initial phase of financial repression, either the cost of borrowing decreases or the price of food increases. Most times, both things occur simultaneously. It is in this initial phase that owning farmland can be a source of wealth. However, financial repression will only finish when governments can no longer succeed at increasing it. As soon as the initial inflationary phase lifts the price of farmland and farmers harvest the benefits of higher commodity prices, governments will set their taxing eyes on them and their immovable wealth. At that point, farmers always wish they were simply commodity traders. While this happens, the uneducated observer is at a loss trying to make sense of rising commodity prices with lower farmland profitability. Usually too, the market for farmland freezes. What really happens though is that, as governments increase taxes, directly or indirectly on farmers, commodity prices rise because farming is no longer profitable. Farmers, at the same time, see this situation as temporary and refuse to sell their lands. In extreme cases, governments end up seizing the land, under the so-called agrarian reforms. There is not one single chapter in the history of financial repressions where this story has not unfolded so. Not one. At the end, when chaos finally sets in with hyperinflation, those farmers who saved their lives and that of their loved ones by leaving everything behind and migrating to another nation will consider themselves fortunate. This was the case in the borders of the Roman Empire, in Ancient Egypt, in the American colonies (with farmers leaving New York State to settle in Upper Canada, today Western Ontario), France in the 1790s or Zimbabwe at the end of the twentieth century.

Bibliography

Masset, Philippe (Lausanne Hotel School) and Weisskopf, Jean-Philippe (University of Fribourg). (March 2010). Raise Your Glass: Wine Investment and the Financial Crisis. *American Association of Wine Economists*. Working Paper 57. Retrieved October 2015 from https://www.researchgate.net/publication/228937213_Raise_your_Glass_Wine_Investment_and_the_Financial_Crisis.

10

Economic Growth

I find no particular reason to link economic growth with democracy. Yet in practice, the explicit search for economic growth, however, belongs to the age of democracy. In the twenty-first century, investors cannot ignore that the main goal of policy makers is to "maximize" economic growth.

But the obvious question is how do we define economic growth? What is economic growth? For a central banker of a developed country in 2016, economic growth can be achieved by monetizing fiscal deficits, which implies it can be gained by transferring wealth between sectors and generations.

But there is also an intellectual battlefield, which we should be aware of. In the next paragraphs I (extremely) briefly walk through the history of the idea of economic growth to this day. I cannot be exhaustive and I encourage you to do further research on the works mentioned below. At the end, I discuss their implications for investing.

When Did This All Begin?

When did the idea of economic growth first appear? The concern with economic growth can be traced to before the French Revolution when the analysis on the distribution of income was first examined.[1] The physiocratic movement, led by Francois Quesnay in 1759, pioneered the debate. Physiocrats reasoned that if agriculture was the basis of economic growth, a distribution

---

[1] According to Nicholas Kaldor, David Ricardo pioneered the theory of distribution. Although Ricardo explicitly says in the preface to his *Principles of Political Economy and Taxation* that "…*To determine the laws which regulate this distribution, is the principal problem in Political Economy*…".

© The Author(s) 2018
M. Arisson, *Investing in the Age of Democracy*,
https://doi.org/10.1007/978-3-319-95903-0_10

of income favouring this sector would be advisable. Below, I show the Tableau Economique, probably the first economic model (designed by Quesnay) (Fig. 10.1).

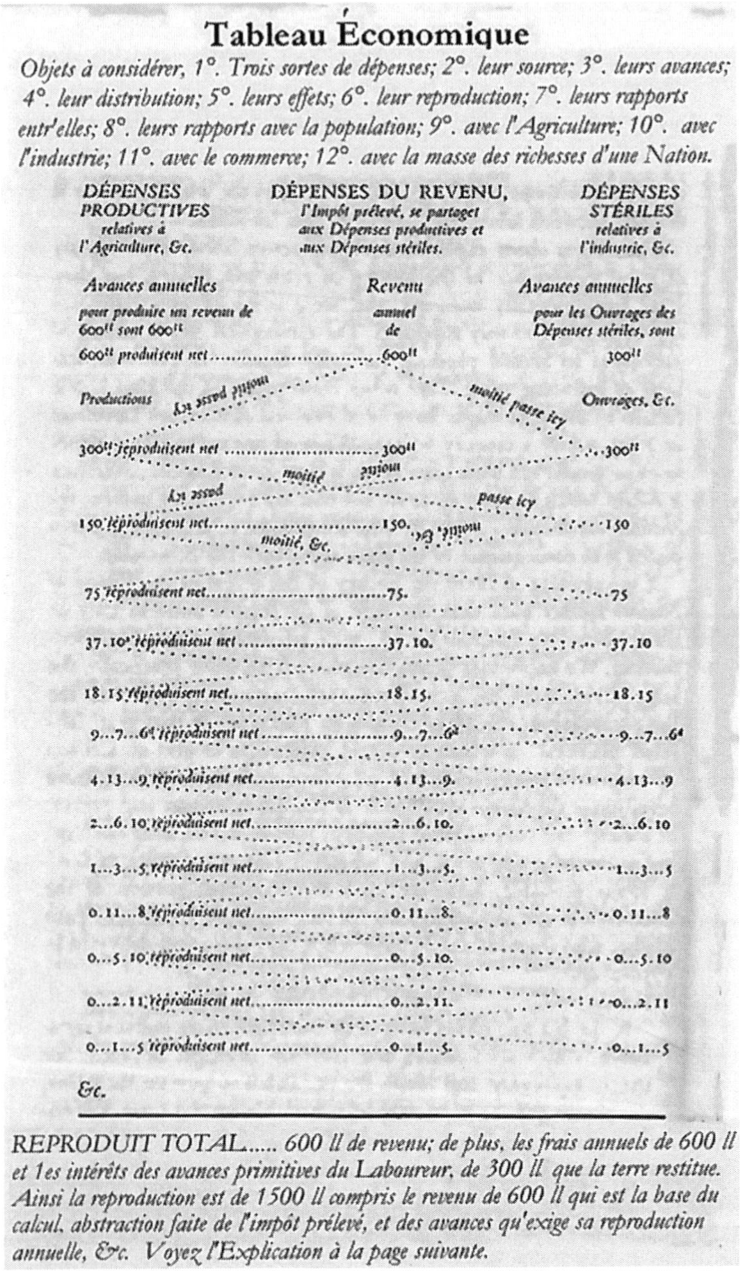

Fig. 10.1 Le Tableau Economique. (Source: Wikimedia Commons)

The idea that there was an "optimal" distribution of income triggered the investigation of what determines the same. Simultaneously and brewed by Thomas Malthus, there was another idea: Full employment requires a growing income. It was on these two pillars (i.e. the distribution of income and the relation between employment and output) that modern thinking on economic growth was born, with the additional analysis of how capital is created. In the following paragraphs, I present a brief commentary about the main research done on economic growth.

Roy F. Harrod

The first "modern" discussion on economic growth is probably that of R. F. Harrod, titled "An Essay in Dynamic Theory", and published in 1939. Harrod's work has historical relevance although it is not original and merely seeks to give Keynes' ideas a dynamic dimension. His main assumptions are that the supply of savings is determined by income (i.e. interest rates play no role, which would have probably made him a good Federal Open Markets Committee member). For Harrod, investment responds to income growth and there is always equilibrium in the savings market. Just like in the rest of the modern discussions on economic growth, monetary aspects are ignored. There is a constant concern—sometimes turned into an obsession—to address equilibrium conditions. These analytic frameworks are Walrasian in structure (discussed in Lesson 1) and ignore the impact of aggregate leverage (from fractional reserve banking) in a credit-based monetary system. I think there is no excuse for this omission, for others were already very aware of its impact in the 1930s. Harrod worked within a single commodity and production factor model, and held that a departure from equilibrium would activate a self-fulfilling, spiralling instability. He anticipates Ben Bernanke and followers when he asserts that to address such instability, policy is required: "... *The ideal policy would be to manipulate the proper warranted rate, so that it should be equal to the natural rate...*" If he sounds familiar, it is no coincidence.

Evsey D. Domar

After World War II, Evsey Domar presented his work "Capital Expansion, Rate of Growth and Employment", in January 1946. Domar incorporated prices into his model, but assumed no fluctuations. Unlike Harrod, he does not require equilibrium in the savings market, but discusses the generation of capital in an economic system. He brought attention to the issue of full employment:

"...*Our first task is to discover...the rate of growth at which the economy* **must** *expand in order to remain in a continuous state of full employment...*" He was not just referring to the employment of labour, but of capital too. In this regard, he precedes John B. Taylor's famous "rule",[2] because he examines the dynamics of the gap between potential and actual output (he actually focused on the relation between change in output and investment, which he called potential social average investment productivity).

James Tobin

Almost a decade later, most economists still assumed that the factors of production were fixed and that the monetary context had no impact on economic growth. James Tobin was to challenge the status quo in a paper titled "A Dynamic Aggregative Model" published in April of 1955, by the *Journal of Political Economy*. For Tobin, economies have constant returns to scale ("...*if labor and capital expand over time in proportion, then output will expand in the same proportion...*"). His innovation is the introduction of "asset preferences" as one more variable affecting economic growth. Tobin assumes that we either hold currency (at zero interest) or real assets. There are no financial assets (i.e. paper that pays a coupon). Inflation or deflation is therefore the product of shifts in our aggregate allocation, between currency and real assets, driven by preferences. For instance, if we decide to hold less currency (i.e. we bid for real assets), there will be inflationary pressures. Interestingly, he realized that technological progress is deflationary, and recommended monetary expansion to offset deflation. His merit was in understanding the implication of said expansion. Tobin tells us that the same "...*cannot be accomplished by monetary policy in the conventional sense but must be the result of deficit financing (...) clearly, such a discussion requires the introduction of additional types of assets, including bank deposits and private debts...*". In other words, he anticipated our current "problem": Lack of collateral, in a credit-based system with shadow banking.[3] Tobin concludes that under such expansion "the normal result is that consumption will be a larger and investment a smaller share of a given level of real income."

---

[2] The Taylor rule, after John Brian Taylor, currently the Mary and Robert Raymond Professor of Economics at Stanford University.

[3] For a good discussion of this system, refer Zerohedge's article "Desperately Seeking $11.2 Trillion In Collateral, Or How "Modern Money" Really Works", May 1, 2013. In July 2017, with the plans to replace Libor with the Broad Treasuries Funding Rate, we could say that, if the plans are confirmed, we will effectively use fiscal deficits to supply currency.

Robert Solow

Robert Solow is "the" name in the theory of economic growth in the twenti-eth century. His work on this field eventually earned him the Nobel Memorial Prize in Economics in 1987. His ground-breaking opus appeared one year after Tobin's, in February 1956, published at the *Quarterly Journal of Economics* and titled "A Contribution to the Theory of Economic Growth". Solow takes Harrod's and Domar's research but abandons the assumption that production takes place under conditions of fixed proportions (between labour and capi-tal), introduces a rate of technological change and incorporates an interest rate-sensitive savings function. Solow's conclusions are powerful and based on the premise that in the long run, our economic system has constant returns to scale. His main conclusion is that full employment (or perhaps I should say, an optimal ratio between labour and capital) is not (as suggested by his prede-cessors and Bernanke) obtained from a key level of output/income, but from a key marginal productivity of capital, which in turn determines the real wage rate. How do we get to that key marginal productivity of capital? Thanks to perfect price flexibility, within a stable monetary system (implied; for those interested, refer eqs. 10–12 of his model). Lastly, Solow incorporates techno-logical progress as an exogenous (i.e. arbitrary, not determined by his model) and neutral variable. It's a pity—in my opinion—that Solow did not explore the monetary aspects implied by his work. His idea of economic growth makes sense under commodity-based money (i.e. no central banking), because one can agree with him on the elasticity of supply of factors (capital and labour, he excludes land) to their respective prices (interest rate and wages). But perhaps if he had done so, he would have been less popular. Solow would become emeritus Institute Professor of Economics at MIT and recently wrote on the ongoing financial crisis.[4]

This was a very brief discussion on economic growth and I discussed only those works I am more familiar with, omitting other important economists (in no particular order), like Hicks, Swan, Robinson, Phelps, Malinvaud, Arrow, Kahn, Kaldor and Sidrauski.

---

[4] *"How to Save American Finance from Itself"*, April 8, 2013, at New Republic: https://newrepublic.com/article/112679/how-save-american-finance-itself

But What Is Economic Growth?

To start, I do not like the term "economic growth", because it is based on a quantitative judgement, which lacks economic sense. Economic growth cannot be measured because it is simply specialization of knowledge. This idea had already been elaborated by Adam Smith. If we act purposefully and relative prices are not intervened, all it takes to improve our standard of living is to allow the social cooperation and coordination processes (also known as "markets") to unfold, allocating resources where they are needed.

The mere concept of income distribution is flawed, as Ludwig von Mises appropriately explained. We do not produce something and then distribute the income generated by its sale. **The distribution of that income is already decided, agreed and precedes production**. And that product is made precisely because of and not in spite of a previously agreed income distribution.

Under free social coordination, unemployment is naturally the result of constant change and creative destruction and it is low. Equilibrium, by necessity, is incompatible with economic growth, because under it no change occurs. It is exactly that constant reallocation of resources carried out by entrepreneurs what increases efficiency and productivity.[5] Hence there is no place for an optimal savings rate or an optimal stock of capital. To allow this coordination to unfold, money and financial assets are indispensable, because they enable social and intertemporal cooperation. Cooperation is what drives specialization and improvements in production methods. Hence, when money dies (under hyperinflation), specialization dies too.

Implications for the Investor

In the twenty-first century and at the time of this publication, central banks seek to materialize their quantitative goal of economic growth via the so-called wealth effect. This effect consists in raising the wealth of those who hold financial assets by lowering their discount rates. Because the lowering of the benchmark rate is obtained with inflation, this policy is a transfer of wealth from those who are poor and cannot afford to save and invest in financial assets to those who have already saved. The richer this latter group is, the higher the wealth transfer is. In other words, this wealth effect is one of the most regressive policies as the rich become richer at the expense of the poor becoming poorer.

---

[5] Not from a mechanistic perspective but from an economic one.

Pro-economic Growth Policies Are Bad News for Investors, but a Dream for Traders Central bankers have their own interpretation of economic growth and it does not fit any of the theoretical developments just discussed. Their twenty-first-century zero or negative interest rate policies have inverted the risk-return relationship in the capital structure forcing banks to strive so hard to get reasonable yield investments that they ended up acting like private equity firms. The elimination of interest rates as signals for resource allocation creates a sea of opportunity for capital structure trades but only confusion for investments. Transactions (i.e. mergers and acquisitions) that permit to raise debt to later distribute a dividend or buyback shares have been the norm post 2008 and, in many cases, successful business models for private equity firms. From a structural perspective, pro-economic growth policies thus push unde- cidable businesses to shift their capital structure from equity to debt, which creates systemic risk. Investors seeking value in the process will only find frustration.

Bibliography

Ricardo, David. (1817). *On the Principles of Political Economy and Taxation.* (1st Edition). London: John Murray. Retrieved July 2013 via Google Books from https://books.google.ca/books?id=cUBKAAAAYAAJ&dq=editions:y8vXR4oK9 R8C&pg=PR1&redir_esc=y#v=onepage&q&f=true

Harrod, R. F. (March 1939). An Essay in Dynamic Theory. *The Economic Journal, XLIX, pp. 14–33.* London: Macmillan and Co. Ltd. Errata (Jun 1939), p. 377.

Domar, Evsey. (April 1946). Capital expansion, rate of growth and employment. *Econometrica, pp. 137–147.*

Tobin, James. (April 1955). A Dynamic Aggregative Model. *Journal of Political Economy, LXIII, No. 2, pp. 103–115.*

Solow, Robert. (February 1956). A Contribution to the Theory of Economic Growth. *The Quarterly Journal of Economics, LXX, pp. 65–94.* Cambridge, MA.: Harvard University Press.

Solow, Robert. (April 2013). How to Save American Finance from Itself. *New Republic.* Retrieved December 2015 from https://newrepublic.com/arti- cle/112679/how-save-american-finance-itself

Bank Charter Act (1844). Retrieved September, 2015, from https://web.archive.org/ web/20101203090327/http://www.bankofengland.co.uk/about/legislation/ 1844act.pdf

Final Comments

It is only natural that, being aware of our mortality, we want to save something for a time when we can no longer work, for our offspring or for any unexpected misfortune. Over the centuries, this natural need spontaneously crystalized in the development of institutions, like life insurance or the real estate market. From the start, modern democracies progressively intervened these natural developments, affecting our ability to save, to the point that today it is almost impossible for the average citizen in a developed nation to have some material control over his future. This impairment took place so slowly that it went unnoticed. It took a few generations, but surely, any of our predecessors living in the early 1900s would easily notice how limited the liberties that we enjoy today are.

This process unfolded through a sequence of diverse and parallel lines. From an economic perspective, it began with the gradual destruction of money, our pivotal institution for social cooperation. The destruction began at the end of 1913,[1] indirectly, leading first to the Great Depression, and later to World War II. The final nail in the coffin was put in 1971 (with Nixon's end to the US dollar convertibility with gold) and at the time of this writing, we are debating whether or not we should do away with cash.

A century into the age of democracy, governments across the globe launched income taxes and mandatory pension plans. These two initiatives have left citizens with minimal income available to save, and together with inflationary policies, they have brought about the largest wealth gap seen in the history of mankind.

---

[1] Some would suggest that it took off earlier: July 19, 1844, with the Peel Act.

© The Author(s) 2018
M. Arisson, *Investing in the Age of Democracy*,
https://doi.org/10.1007/978-3-319-95903-0

Fast forward to the beginning of the twenty-first century and we witness the complete destruction of the institution of debt as a vehicle to invest our savings, because nominal interest rates are either nil or negative and we are pushed to allocate whatever resources we have left, in public markets. Because these changes were gradual and took place across generations, those of us living today have lost the ability to save and the skills necessary to invest. The goal of this book was to rediscover those skills and accordingly suggest a way to approach investing.

Democracy was rediscovered and promoted globally by the coordinated effort of intellectuals in Western Europe and North America. This is important because, while our liberties were systematically limited later on, the intellectual roots of this political movement ensured that at least science and the scientific method would remain relatively unscathed. The consequence of this asymmetry between social and scientific freedoms is counterintuitive: After the French and American revolutions, material progress continued to unfold steadily, and the productivity gained afforded us a cushion against the distortions caused by central planning. This was more visible at the end of the twentieth century when the disruption caused by the internet and information technologies were so powerful that even with negative interest rates and confiscatory taxation; we still manage to improve our living conditions.

The support for science has been dogmatic, however. It was applied to all fields of interest, including the social sciences. The result was an indiscriminate use of infinitesimal calculus, general equilibrium models and probability theory to study phenomena that are neither of a continuous nor stable or stochastic nature. Yet, thousands of people working every day in the financial sector apply these methods without thinking. And every few years, not even a decade, we see with indifference wealth lost to leveraged trades based on such methods. The answer so far has been more regulation and more central planning.

In light of the above, what is one left to do? We cannot afford not to act. Success at investing will always be based on discipline and method. The first step is to understand our liquidity needs and intertemporal preferences. In this manner, we will not be unnecessarily paying a premium to keep our savings liquid and we will have a sense of proportion, of perspective, on what we can achieve and must be achieved. The future value of a compounded dollar grows exponentially with time and contrary to popular wisdom, the younger we are the more we must favour simple interest rate compounding at the expense of other investments or trades.

There is no neutrality in capital structure decisions and information is not free or equally available to all of us. For this reason, we must always avoid placing our savings in public securities and seek to retain maximum control over them, to be able to deal with uncertain events, as they appear. And appear they will.

Once we identify a business theme we like, we must make a judgement call and assess how undecidable it is. The fit between decidability and your choice of capital structure is critical.[2]

Simultaneously with the choice of business theme, we must consider the institutional context surrounding the investment tool we choose versus its ontological nature and that of the business chosen. The typical question that brings the institutional consistency of an investment is simply this: "Does this investment vehicle make sense?" As well, we need to understand the monetary and institutional situation that the relevant central bank (i.e. that of the currency zone the business is in) faces.

After all the considerations above, if we are still inclined to allocating a portion of our savings to a specific opportunity, we must determine if the same is in a capital asset or not. If it is, we will be investing. If it is not, we will be trading. In the latter case, we must identify an exit situation, with a stop exit. Under both cases, we must ex ante also determine a stop loss. In all cases, we must execute accordingly, and without hesitation.

If it is not possible for us to avoid the public securities markets, I suggest considering two alternative options:

First, because we would be at the mercy of insiders protected by limited liability, we must make proper use of the theory of probability. We must diversify enough so that the return we look for behaves as stochastically as possible. This means that the collective of the asset class chosen should exhibit a trend converging to a floor return and that same trend should present itself regardless of the time horizon selected.

A second alternative is to select the stock of a public company that is so undecidable that not even its management can claim to know better than you what the future holds for the business. But because said stock will probably not pay a dividend (if it does, you're doing something wrong), you will not be investing. You will be trading.

Finally, these allocations in public securities, if possible, should be insured against a liquidity crisis. The vehicle for that is an out-of-the-money option-like instrument directly linked to the funding market in the currency zone relevant to your investment. In Canada, between 2013 and 2017, that instrument was the exchange rate of the Canadian versus the US dollar (i.e. long USDCAD).

Morten Arisson

---

[2] A useful rule of thumb, I think, is to understand the accounting rules around its business model, particularly the measurement of revenue. A business whose accounting rules are (legitimately, not driven by fraud) evolving is undecidable. Think of the early years of the internet, when clicks, searches and visits where part of the group of metrics used by investors to determine potential profitability.

Bibliography

Anonymous. (May 1, 2013). *Desperately Seeking $11.2 Trillion In Collateral, Or How "Modern Money" Really Works*. Retrieved from https://www.zerohedge.com/news/2013-05-01/desperately-seeking-112-trillion-collateral-or-how-modern-money-really-works

Aristotle. (n.d.). *Politics*. University of Chicago Press, Mar. 29, 2013. Retrieved from Google Books June 2015 from https://books.google.ca/books?id=DJP44GomyNoC&lpg=PP1&pg=PP1#v=onepage&q&f=false

Artzrouni, Marc. (2009). *The Mathematics of Ponzi Schemes*. Dept. of Mathematics, University of Pau. Retrieved October 2015 from https://mpra.ub.uni-muenchen.de/14420/1/

Banco Central de la República Argentina, Informe Semanal de Subastas de Lebacs and Nobacs, April 11–15, 2016.

Bank for International Settlements, Monetary and Economic Department. Developing corporate bond markets in Asia. *BIS Papers No 26: Proceedings of a BIS/PBC seminar held in Kunming, China on 17–18 November 2005*. Released February 2006 and Retrieved May 2015 from https://www.bis.org/publ/bppdf/bispap26.pdf

Basel Committee on Banking Supervision. (May 31 2001). Operational Risk Consultative Document. Ch. V. Retrieved May 2015 from https://www.fsa.go.jp/inter/bis/bj_20010117_1/1n.pdf

Bastos Boubeta, Miguel Anxo. (2013). *Libertarianismo y Conservadurismo*. VIII Universidad de Verano, Instituto Juan de Mariana. Retrieved August 2015 from https://youtu.be/NzZJipDVd9o

Bastos Boubeta, Miguel Anxo. (July 2015). *Política Exterior Liberal*. Presentation at the X Universidad de Verano, Instituto Juan de Mariana, Lanzarote. Retrieved October 2015 from https://youtu.be/Zt7CfsNh3EQ?t=24m43s

© The Author(s) 2018
M. Arisson, *Investing in the Age of Democracy*,
https://doi.org/10.1007/978-3-319-95903-0

Benes, Jaromir, and Kumhof, Michael (August 2012). The Chicago Plan Revisited. *IMF Working Paper*. WP 12/202. Washington, DC: International Monetary Fund. Retrieved November 2013 from http://www.imf.org/external/pubs/ft/wp/2012/wp12202.pdf

Bernoulli, Jakob. (1713). *Ars Conjectandi. Pars Quarta tradens Usum & Applicationem Praecedentis Doctrinae in Civilibus, Moralibues & Oeconomicis.* Translated into English by Oskar Cheinine, Berlin 2005. Retrieved September 2015 from http://www.sheynin.de/download/bernoulli.pdf

Brown, Brendan. (March 2013). *The Global Curse of the Federal Reserve: How Its Monetary Virus Stimulates Destructive Waves of Irrational Exuberance and Depression.* Murray N. Rothbard Memorial Lecture, presented at the Austrian Economics Research Conference, Auburn, AL. Retrieved March 2013 from https://www.youtube.com/watch?v=INDZe4KAZS4&feature=youtu.be&t=19m

Cobb, Charles W. (Amherst College) and Douglas, Paul H. (Univ. Of Chicago). (March 1928). A Theory of Production. *The American Economic Review*. Vol. 18, No. 1, Supplement, Papers and Proceedings of the Fortieth Annual Meeting of the American Economic Association, pp. 139. Retrieved January 2015 from http://www.jstor.org/stable/1811556?seq=1#page_scan_tab_contents

Cummings, Lewis Vance. (1940). *Alexander the Great.* New York, NY: Grove Press, 1968.

David, Florence N. (1909). *Games, Gods and Gambling: A History of Probability and Statistical Ideas.* Mineola, NY: Dover Publications Inc., 1988.

Draghi, Mario, President of the European Central Bank. (2016). *Addressing the causes of low interest rates.* Introductory speech held at a panel on "*The future of financial markets: A changing view of Asia*" at the Annual Meeting of the Asian Development Bank, Frankfurt am Main, 2 May 2016. Retrieved May 2016 from https://www.ecb.europa.eu/press/key/date/2016/html/sp160502.en.html

Ferguson, Niall. (2008). The Ascent of Money. New York, NY: The Penguin Press.

Fernholz, Robert and Karatzas, Ioannis. (2008). *Stochastic Portfolio Theory: an Overview.* Retrieved September 2015 from http://www.math.columbia.edu/~ik/FernKarSPT.pdf

Gaarder Haug, Espen and Taleb, Nassim N. (2010). *Option traders use (very) sophisticated heuristics, never the Black-Scholes-Merton formula. Journal of Economic Behavior & Organization.* Volume 77, Issue 2, February 2011, Pages 97–106.

Gács, Peter (Boston University) and Lovász, László (Yale University). (Spring 1999). *Complexity of Algorithms.* Lecture Notes. Retrieved March 2013 from http://web.cs.elte.hu/~lovasz/complexity.pdf

Gaxotte, Pierre. (1970). *La Révolution Française.* Paris: Éditions Tallandier, 2014.

Grasselli, M. R. and Hurd, T. R. (McMaster University, January 2010). *Credit Risk Modeling.* Hamilton, ON, Canada. Retrieved May 2015 from https://ms.mcmaster.ca/~grasselli/Credittext2011.pdf

Group of Ten. (May 31st 1965). *Report of the study group on the creation of reserve assets.* Report to the Deputies of The Group of Ten. Retrieved April 2013 from http://www.bis.org/publ/gten_b.pdf

Grotius, H. (1583–1645). *De Iure belli ac pacis* 2.11.13. Digitized by the Internet Archive in 2008 with funding from Microsoft Corporation. Retrieved July 2015 from https://archive.org/details/hugonisgrottiide010grotuoft

Hoppe, Hans-Hermann. (Spring 2007). The Limits of Numerical Probability: Frank H. Knight and Ludwig Von Mises and the Frequency Interpretation. *The Quarterly Journal of Austrian Economics.* Vol. 10, No. 1: 3–21. Retrieved September 2015 from https://mises-media.s3.amazonaws.com/qjae10_1_1.pdf?file=1&type=document

Huerta de Soto, Jesús. (2006). *Dinero, Crédito Bancario y Ciclos Económicos.* Madrid: Unión Editorial, 6ta Edición, 2016.

Huerta de Soto, Jesús. (2008a). *Market Order and Entrepreneurial Creativity.* Cheltenham, UK: Edward Elgar Publishing.

Huerta de Soto, Jesús. (2008b). *The Austrian School: Market Order and Entrepreneurial Creativity.* Cheltenham, UK: Edward Elgar Publishing Ltd.

Huerta de Soto, Jesús. (2014). *Ensayos de Economía Política.* Madrid: Unión Editorial.

Hull, John. (1996). *Options, Futures, and Other Derivatives.* Third Edition. Upper Saddle River, NJ: Prentice Hall.

Investigations of Economic Problems, Hearings before the Committee on Finance, United States Senate, Seventy-Second Congress, Second Session, Pursuant to S. Res. 315, February 13 to 28, 1933.

Johnston, David. (June 1995). Limiting Liability: Roman Law and the Civil Law Tradition. *Chicago-Kent Law Review.* Vol. 70, Issue 4. Symposium on Ancient Law, Economics & Society, Part I: The Development of Law in Classical and Early Medieval Europe. Article 6. Retrieved September 2016 from https://scholarship.kentlaw.iit.edu/cgi/viewcontent.cgi?article=2998&context=cklawreview

Keynes, John Maynard. (1921). *Treatise on Probability.* London: Macmillan & Co., Ltd.

Landro, Alberto. Acerca de la existencia del verdadero valor de una probabilidad. *Revista de Economía Política de Buenos Aires.* Año 4, Vols. 7 y 8 (2010a): 221–245. Retrieved September 2015 from http://ojs.econ.uba.ar/ojs/index.php/REPBA/article/view/258/464

Landro, Alberto. Acerca del "Regellosigkeitsaxiom" de Von Mises. *Cuadernos del CIMBAGE* Nro. 12 (2010b): 1–21. Retrieved September 2015 from http://ojs.econ.uba.ar/ojs/index.php/CIMBAGE/article/view/351/640

Lewis, Michael. (2014). *Flash Boys.* New York: W.W. Norton & Company Ltd.

Li, Chi. (1922). *Some Anthropological Problems of China.* Baltimore: Chinese Students' Monthly. Page 327.

Malmendier, Ulrike. (2008). *Law and Finance "at the Origin".* Retrieved September 2016 from https://eml.berkeley.edu/~ulrike/Papers/JELDraft70.pdf

Malmendier, Ulrike. (2002). *Societas Publicanorum, Staatliche Wirtschaftsactivitätenin den Händen privater Unternehmer.* Böhlau Verlag.

Malmendier, Ulrike. (n.d.). *Publicani*. Retrieved August 2016 from: https://eml.berkeley.edu/~ulrike/Papers/Publicani_Article_v5.pdf

Markowitz, Harry. (March 1952). Portfolio Selection. *The Journal of Finance*. Vol. 7, No. 1.

Marshall, Alfred. (1890). *Principles of Economics*. London: Palgrave Classics in Economics, Eighth Edition.

Masset, Philippe (Lausanne Hotel School) and Weisskopf, Jean-Philippe (University of Fribourg). (March 2010). Raise Your Glass: Wine Investment and the Financial Crisis. *American Association of Wine Economists*. Working Paper 57. Retrieved October 2015 from https://www.researchgate.net/publication/228937213_Raise_your_Glass_Wine_Investment_and_the_Financial_Crisis

Menger, Carl. (1892–1909). Collected Works of Carl Menger (in German). Volume IV. London: London School of Economics and Political Science, 1936. Retrieved August 2015 from https://mises-media.s3.amazonaws.com/Collected%20Works%20of%20Carl%20Menger%20%28in%20German%29%20Volume%20IV_5.pdf?file=1&type=document

Modigliani, F. and Miller, M. (June 1958). The Cost of Capital, Corporation Finance and the Theory of Investment. *American Economic Review*. Vol. 48, No. 3, pp. 261–297.

Plutarch. (75 A.C.E.). *Lycurgus*. Translated by John Dryden. Retrieved May 2015 via The Internet Classics Archive from http://classics.mit.edu/Plutarch/lycurgus.html

Poisson, Siméon Denis. (1837). *Recherches sur la probabilité des jugements en matière criminelle et en matière civile, précédées des règles générales du calcul des probabilités*. Paris: Bachelier Imprimeur-Libraire. Retrieved August 2015 from https://www-liphy.ujf-grenoble.fr/pagesperso/bahram/Phys_Stat/Biblio/Poisson_Proba_1838.pdf

Rodgers, Mary Tone and Wilson, Berry K. (Summer 2011). Systemic Risk, Missing Gold Flows and the Panic of 1907. *The Quarterly Journal of Austrian Economics*. Vol 14, No. 2, pp. 158–187.

Rodríguez, Carlos Alfredo. (September 1993). Economic Consequences of Quasi-Fiscal Deficits. *CEMA Working Papers*. No. 91. Retrieved May 2014 from https://www.ucema.edu.ar/publicaciones/download/documentos/91.pdf

Rosenberg, Jeffrey. (February 5, 2010). Default (even a sovereign one) is a liquidity event. *US Fixed Income Situation, Fixed Income Strategy*. Bank of America.

Rueff, Jacques. (1971). *Le péché monétaire de l'Occident*. Chapitre XI, p. 177. Paris: CD Librairie Plon.

Russell, Bertrand. (1922). *The Problem of China*. London: George Allen & Unwin Ltd.

Russell, Bertrand. (1946). *History of Western Philosophy*. London: Unwin University Books.

Sanguinetti, Horacio. (1986). *Curso de Derecho Político*. Buenos Aires: Editorial Astrea, 4ta Edición, 2000.

Sardone, Sergio. (2012). Los secuestros de las remesas americanas de particulares de Carlos V a través de los notarios sevillanos. *Temas Americanistas*, Número 29, pp. 21–64.

Seghezza, E. (2008). *The Genoa Conference and the Gold Exchange Standard.* Università di Genova, Disefin working paper, no. 7.

Shafer, Glenn. (1996). The Significance of Jacob Bernoulli's Ars Conjectandi for the Philosophy of Probability Today. *Journal of Econometrics.* vol. 75, No. 1, 15–32.

Sibileau, Martin. (2014). *Formalizing Austrian Thought: A suggested approach.* Madrid: Revista Procesos de Mercardo, Año 2014, Vol. 11, No. 2.

Sibileau, Martin. (November 2012). Why The Chicago Plan is flawed reasoning and would fail. *A View from the Trenches.* Retrieved November 2013 from https://www.zerohedge.com/news/2012-11-11/guest-post-why-chicago-plan-flawed-reasoning-and-would-fail

Smith, Adam. (1776). *An Inquiry into the Nature and Causes of the Wealth of Nations. (Book V, Chapter I).* Edinburgh: Thomas Nelson, 1843. Retrieved July 2015 via Google Books from https://books.google.ca/books?id=8k_K8rf2fnUC&pg=PA5#v=onepage&q&f=false

Statement of William McChesney Martin, Jr., Chairman, Board of Governors of the Federal Reserve System, before the Subcommittee on National Security and International Operations of the Committee on Government Operations United States Senate Aug. 30, 1965. Retrieved May 2013 from https://fraser.stlouisfed.org/files/docs/historical/martin/martin65_0830.pdf

Voet, Johannis. (1716). *Commentarius*, 14.1.5. European Libraries Collection, digitized by Google from the National Library of Naples. Retrieved July 2015 from https://ia800200.us.archive.org/10/items/bub_gb_ap8ZayGxPbwC/bub_gb_ap8ZayGxPbwC.pdf

Von Mises, Ludwig. (1949). *Human Action: A Treatise on Economics.* Auburn, AL: Ludwig von Mises Institute, Scholar's Edition, 1998.

Von Mises, Richard. (1928). *Probability, Statistics and Truth.* Second revised English Edition, prepared by Hilda Geiringer. Mineola, NY: Dover Publications, Inc. Second revised English Edition, 1981.

Walras, Léon. (1926). *Éléments d'Économie Politique Pure ou Théorie de la Richesse Sociale.* Edition définitive revue et augmentée par l'auteur. Paris: H. Pichon et R. Durand-Auzias Éditeurs.

Ricardo, David. (1817). *On the Principles of Political Economy and Taxation.* (1st Edition). London: John Murray. Retrieved July 2013 via Google Books from https://books.google.ca/books?id=cUBKAAAAYAAJ&dq=editions:y8vXR4oK9R8C&pg=PR1&redir_esc=y#v=onepage&q&f=true

Harrod, R. F. (March 1939). An Essay in Dynamic Theory. *The Economic Journal, XLIX, pp. 14–33.* London: Macmillan and Co. Ltd. Errata (Jun. 1939), p. 377.

Domar, Evsey. (April 1946). Capital expansion, rate of growth and employment. *Econometrica, pp. 137–147.*

Tobin, James. (April 1955). A Dynamic Aggregative Model. *Journal of Political Economy, LXIII, No. 2, pp. 103–115.*

Solow, Robert. (February 1956). A Contribution to the Theory of Economic Growth. *The Quarterly Journal of Economics, LXX, pp. 65–94.* Cambridge, MA: Harvard University Press.

Solow, Robert. (April 2013). How to Save American Finance from Itself. *New Republic.* Retrieved December 2015 from https://newrepublic.com/article/112679/how-save-american-finance-itself

Bank Charter Act (1844). Retrieved September 2015 from https://web.archive.org/web/20101203090327/http://www.bankofengland.co.uk/about/legislation/1844act.pdf

Index[1]

---

[1] Note: Page numbers followed by 'n' refer to notes.

M. Arisson, *Investing in the Age of Democracy*,
https://doi.org/10.1007/978-3-319-95903-0

Printed in Great Britain
by Amazon